BARBARA POWELL

Finding Leadville

My Story to a Hallowed 100 Mile Finish Line

First edition

ISBN (paperback): 979-8-218-73311-7
ISBN (hardcover): 9798264449789

Editing by Blair Parke

This book was professionally typeset on Reedsy.
Find out more at reedsy.com

To all the women who endure. And to the little girl that lives in each of them. She matters.

To love yourself as you are is a miracle, and to seek yourself is to have found yourself, for now. And now is all we have, and love is who we are.

Anne Lamott

Acknowledgments

Thank you to everyone who made the race and summer of 2023 possible.

Thank you to Greg, my run coach and steadfast believer in what's possible for me. Hallie, my dear, incredible friend, and Cindi, my crew captain. Trapper, my pacer. Cody, my strength coach at America's Highest Gym in Alma and Molly of Zen Ren Massage in Fairplay. Jen, Brie, and Ryan, my coaching colleagues. My sweet friends Sam, Iona, and Erica for cheering me on from afar. Don, Colorado local and established ultrarunner, for his wisdom and care. Lisa, my Life Time support. Val, Lyndsay, and Marnie of the Life Time Foundation. For everyone who donated their hard-earned money and raised me up with their good vibes. The runners of Breckenridge Run Club, including Susan and Tracy, for sharing their trails and friendship. Colleen for the bravery and Tucker for the roommate camaraderie. To the Life Time Foundation as a whole for giving me a strong sense of purpose going into this race.

My fellow racers of the 2023 Leadville 100, Silver Rush 50, Colorado Trail Ragnar, and Leadville Marathon. The town of Leadville for hosting us all, and to Tamara, the race director. Ken, Merilee, and Cole Chlouber for the family feel at the start and finish line.

My family, especially my nieces and nephews, for sending me sweet notes of encouragement. Both of my parents for doing their best and attempting to share their greatest treasure of Catholicism with me. My father, for the true gift of connection to nature. My sister Sarah for the almost weekly check-ins while I was huffing and puffing at altitude. My sisters Evelyn and Gina for their love and support. Joe, my Irish Twin, who taught me about creative thought and compelling storytelling. Rob, the brother with thoughtful insight and important questions as I first released a chapter at a time online.

To those first readers who followed along, a chapter at a time, on my website; you know who you are, and you're wonderful. Mike for his tenderness as he edited my messy "I-thought-I-was-done-but-far-from-it" draft. Eugene for his thoughts on an even messier draft. Skye and Jon for the Minnesota run-buddy hype as I wrote this over the year. Blair for the masterful edits and suggestions: you helped me shape this manuscript into a real book.

All of my clients who inspire me by wanting to explore deeper versions of themselves and grow into the people they desire to become. Every story matters and I am honored to be a part of shaping yours.

The two-mile-high town of Alma and the brilliant city of Leadville for welcoming me for the summer. Other amazing Colorado stops, including Buena Vista, Salida, Fairplay, Breckenridge and Frisco.

The voices of Mother Teresa and Desmond Tutu who found their way into my pack and onto my bookshelf.

The women who know deep healing and who've held emotional pain, yet choose to keep moving forward.

The younger versions of me who kept going even when it was hard—you brought me here. I love you fiercely. You are celebrated and adored. It was not your fault.

And of course, Chris. My sweet man. I love you. Thank you for letting me go and then cheering me on, right when I need you. You gave me space to live out this Colorado adventure; you gifted me with the creative inspiration to complete this book. Running moves me; music moves you; together we move forward. You taught me what it looks like to remain steadfast, even in the most difficult times Thank you for every time you reminded me: "We can do hard things, honey." I am safe and loved with you.

May we all feel important. May we all chase dreams that are worth having. May we be happy, healthy, and know peace.

And you, the reader. This story is mine, but it may have echoes of yours. I hope it gives you permission to witness and tell your own story, no matter what start or finish line you have in your sight line.

Thank you for spending time with me and my pages.

Introduction

Ten thousand feet in the clouds, and I was running down a mountainside.

Well, maybe you could call it *running,* given the context.

It was nearing the middle of the Leadville 100 trail run, and I was about to pull into the Winfield Aid Station, which marked the official turnaround at mile fifty for the out-and-back course. Wearing daffodil-yellow shorts and a circus-pink tank top, I pulled a custom-made hat over my face to protect it from an unforgiving alpine sun. The bubblegum print, saying *My First Rodeo,* was scrawled in cursive threading above the gracious brim. My back was hunched, equipped with a pack that held a water bladder, now-limp bottles for liquid nutrition, and several crinkled, sticky packages of long-ago consumed gels. Aspen trees rustled their coin dollar leaves as I passed them by, tambourines of shimmering green quaking alongside the trail.

I was, at least, moving downhill on the trail faster than when I was going up. But it felt and looked more like a hobble. My head tilted, as though looking up fully would cause the nearing aid station to draw farther away from me. My feet begged for relief, opting to rebel by becoming heavier as I went further. I had ignored them the entirety of Hope Pass, a climb to 12,000 feet and back down again. Paying any attention to something that will only keep hurting is like rewarding a dog for bad behavior— it'll just make it worse. Now, aware that reprieve was nearby, my feet were defiant as ever.

A beep from my watch prompted me to check my wrist: fifty miles. Fingers grasped white around the trusted trekking poles, and I willed my feet to keep following the directions of the day: Just keep moving.

Step, step, pole, pole.

Step, step, pole, pole.

What are you doing, a thought crept in, *Why are you even out here?*

The air was thin. Each foot scuffle kicked up dust on the old dirt road, caking my once-wet socks from the earlier creek crossing. *The creek crossing.* That seemed like a lifetime ago—a lifetime before I crawled my way to 12,500 feet in the sky, and the last time I saw my crew before the Hope Pass saga began.

The sky was a brilliant blue, nary a cloud. Flashes of the morning's hubbub ricocheted through my mind: excited chatter at the start line and hugging my partner, Chris; the tilt of the shotgun toward the stars; the whooping shuffle of runners taking off from 6th Street toward the wilderness. The wonder I held and the curiosity that bubbled in me. The hope I felt—now a balloon that had lost some air during the long day. Already a series of memories.

How the hell am I going to turn around and do it all again?

A shuttle idled on the dirt road a few yards beyond the aid station. Its doors were open, daring each of us haggard souls to use our remaining strength to crawl inside, lay our bodies to rest, to call it quits. Cots flanked the opposing side of the road, their sturdiness and promise of respite one of the most appealing things I could lay eyes on. Forcing my awareness away from the shuttle, I collapsed onto one of the cots instead.

Looking down, I took in the power of my body: the swell of quads, blue veins working beneath skin, and the heave of lungs in the chest. Pieces of hair stuck to my cheek, and sweat had long ago dried into salted flakes of white on my skin. My eyes brimmed with tears.

I thought of how far my body—and mind—had come. I thought of the summer of training I just surpassed and the lifetime of carrying the little girl in me to this very place in time. It was a disservice to question all of that now. She nudged me — that little girl — and I kept shuffling toward the aid station. Belief, a small wisp turning into a plumage of smoke, swirled around me. My headphones were still in my ears, and instruments with their accompanying vocals throbbed inside my skull.

No matter how I felt, I was a powerful being, making her way through the clouds, on foot. The act of feeling it all—every bump, bruise, ache and twinge—meant I was alive. The mere act of it all meant I was embodying a belief, bringing it to life, and allowing it to grow into a mighty new reality. I was going to turn my ass around, leave this midpoint aid station, and return to downtown Leadville before the thirty-hour clock ran out.

"Fucking watch me," I whistled through my teeth. "I'm doing this." A prayer, an intention, a knowing, a desire. Call it what you will—it was a spoken agreement I continued to make with the trails of Leadville during the most difficult race of my life. An agreement I made with little Barbara ages ago to be strong, to take up space.

I knew I was going to carry my body all the way back—another fifty miles—to where this race had all begun in downtown Leadville.

1

Negotiating

"No,"
said my body,
"we're too tired today."
"No,"
said my mind,
"we deserve to simply stay."
"Let's go,"
said my heart,
"I can't wait
to remember why
sweat and wind
and jagged breath
make us feel like
we can fly."

2

The Night Before the Leadville 100

"Bite off more than you can chew. And chew it." - Ella Williams

Wide-eyed and heart pounding, I lay on my side on the creaky motel bed; the start line to the Leadville 100 was a mere three blocks away from our motel. My partner Chris was snoring peacefully beside me, the lucky bastard. I turned over, pulling my knees up and wrapping my arms around a flattened pillow.

Attempting to relax, I tried out some breathing exercises.

Inhale for four. Hold for four. Exhale for four. Hold. Repeat.

This was about to happen — my first-ever hundred-mile race. *Who do I think I am?* I thought for a brief moment, a familiar echo to actions that out-sized what the world taught me I could be.

My brain was trying to trick me. Another thought rose up: *Why*

6

you? What makes you so special?

Inhale. Hold. Exhale. Repeat. *You chose to be here. You trained to be here. You deserve to be here.*

A silver chain with Thor's hammer glinted on my nightstand, a gift from my impressive friend Trapper who would pace me the final thirty miles the next day. He was someone who naturally lifted others up toward their potential and I found that motivating. This memento was a vote of confidence in me. After our team meeting earlier in the day — my pacer and my crew talking over logistics of the race — he slipped the gift in my hand before engulfing me in a bear hug. It glimmered there on my bedside table, catching moonlight from the crack in the curtains.

You deserve this moment just like anyone else. The inner pep talk surged, and I forced my mind to comprehend. Rolling the updated thoughts around like marbles, warming them up with repetition: *I deserve this moment, too.*

It's easy to get scared about a race like this. Our nervous system has only experienced so much in our lifetimes, so anything new to our physical being can activate all kinds of fight or flight responses. It's inevitable; it's how we change and grow. The body tries to keep you safe at status quo, in the sameness you've always known. Breaking free from that flips the switch, activates the mind, and sends out our very own SOS signals. And my SOS signals were pretty loud that night.

When we hear who we are supposed to be over and over again,

doing otherwise is a sacred act of rebellion. All my life, I had heard — either directly or indirectly — that I was supposed to be a lady, a "good girl." Raised Catholic, I was supposed to sit still, be quiet, act with grace, and let the boys win. I heard it all: Don't burp; always cross your legs and cover your knees. Don't be a slut; save yourself for your husband; listen to your father; behave; and tell your sins to a priest. I was supposed to be the one on the sidelines, cheering on and supporting and loving. I was supposed to be the one holding back, laying low, being quiet, and full of grace. In the end, I was supposed to be small, out of the way, not asking for much.

The sheets got tangled up in my limbs. I peeled them out from between my calves, lightly damp from my stress sweat. I was beginning to realize the enormity I had placed on the big race the next day. The entire summer, and even the years leading up to this, I envisioned myself at this iconic start line in a body that was sharp, strong, and ready. And the eve was finally here.

I remembered, loud and clear, why I was in Leadville.

I was in Leadville as a small but mighty act of rebellion. As an embodiment of my strength. As a reminder of what the body is capable of when she is safe, protected, and nurtured. There had been enough in my life that fooled me into thinking I was anything but those things. This race was my way of showing up for the many parts of me that deserved to feel all those things — especially strong and safe in my own body.

OK, Barbara, I thought in the third person. I clipped on the small bedside lamp. Reaching for my journal and a pen, I scooted my body upward and rested the flat pillow on my lap, setting my notebook on top. Chris grumbled softly.

Time to mind-dump and see what's here.

I began to write:

Running has always been a part of me.

I've been a runner since I was a preteen. I saw my siblings go for runs and I wanted that, too. I wanted the freedom; I loved the fire, the competition, the sweat, and the challenge. I got kind of good. I liked it. It became part of me — an extension of my legs and heart. High school running was so pure, so real. College running got complicated: I got injured; I discovered alcohol; I was out on my own for the first time. But damn, running never left me — it's stayed right with me through the years.

Remember? Traveling from Chicago to Texas in a van full of running shoes with a college friend, Darcy. What a blast! We met up with prestigious cross-country teams, spent the week training with them, took footage of their workouts. I learned what heart could look like from those kids. I felt so much purpose alongside them.

But I also remember being a scared 22-year-old then. There was no guarantee what life would look like after that contract was up. There were no certainties that this job would take me anywhere meaningful or definite as a next step. But hell, I said yes anyway — even when scared, even when I didn't know what would come of it all, didn't I? I said yes anyway.

I pressed the back of my head against the creaky wooden wall, side-eyeing Chris as he continued to snore, trusting the direction of my scribbles: *There's always been someone courageous inside of me, huh?*

I kept on writing.

Even when I'm scared, and I don't know the answer, the outcome, the possibilities — I still get to try. I still get to say yes to myself.

My handwriting sprawled, as though the thoughts leapt through the pen:

I am alive and well, even when I have zero idea what is going to take place tomorrow. It's the journey anyway, isn't it? Because once you say "yes," even when you're scared, that's when something new, different, and potentially life-changing happens for you.

I gulped in air and sent it out with a whispered whoosh.

I don't have to be lady-like out there. I'm not here to be a "good girl." I can be anyone I want to be. So, I can and will be fierce. I can and I will be present in each step. I can and I will finish this fucking thing.

Satisfied, I closed my notebook and set it next to the Thor hammer. There, in a small colorful pile, was a collection of hand-drawn cards from my nieces and nephews. I traced my fingers on a penciled drawing of me at a finish line from my niece — here I was, setting an example of what a woman can do and how she can think, what she can believe. I was showing my

10

family what can be accomplished when Auntie discarded the old story lines and created new ones that served her. There was a weightiness to it; a grand sense of purpose flooded through me.

Pressing my hand to my heart, I accepted the responsibility: I was in Leadville to embody my power. No one can take that from me. No religion, no person, no egregious act of control over me. Not the patriarchy, not Catholicism, not the voice in my own mind that tried to slow me down or stop me.

I was here to embody my power.

Once again, like I had done many times that summer, I brought to mind my younger self. I typically imagined her as the seven year old me in 1995: a small gap between her two front teeth, a playful smile, and an ease in her body that would slowly stiffen over time. She would go on to grapple with God, religion, girlhood, and her body. She would hear a lot of what was expected of her as a young woman growing up in Catholicism. And devastatingly, she would have moments of feeling deeply unsafe in her body.

But here I was now. We were together in Leadville. She was safe with me. And I got to go out there and show her what was possible when we feel safe.

Clicking off the night light, I pulled a sleep mask over my eyes and curled into the warmth of my partner's body.

In that quiet Leadville room, my mind settled, my breath

slowed, and my body found a deep and restful four hours of sleep. It wasn't much, but it was just enough to get me to that start line.

My body had been through so much in my life so far. It was ready to take on the trails through the clouds, and I was ready to take it on for the little girl inside of me. And for all the parts of me that once didn't feel safe and now needed me, more than ever, to be strong.

3

Where I Come From

I grew up on a beautiful dead-end street in small-town Western Massachusetts next door to a sprawling green golf course and an ever-roaring Air Reserve.

On a piece of colonial farmland, I was the middle child of twelve kids, born into an Irish-Welsh-English Catholic home. With five brothers and six sisters, I had a surplus of playmates: Evelyn and Joe, my siblings just older than me by one and two years, and Sarah, my sibling just younger by a year, were especially inseparable. Barefoot with loosened hair and scabby knees, we ran all over our property for hours on end, playing out imaginative stories beneath an endless puffy-cloud sky. We didn't return home from our mini adventures until the rusty dinner bell, hanging on my father's wood working shed, clanged for dinnertime. Only then did we scurry back to wash up and eat.

Not only were there twelve children under roof, but many an animal, too. Dad once worked with a small town veterinarian as a late teen and appreciated having animals of his own. Before my time, a horse or two lived in our barn, followed by a selection of chickens and a rooster. Two Newfoundlands ran inside and out regularly in my childhood, crashing into us children with an unyielding joy only found in dogs. A couple of parakeets lived briefly in a suspended cage by the front window, along with a gecko upstairs in the boys' room. A new litter of barn cats arrived every summer, creating a rallying game of seek when we realized that the pregnant mother cat Ginny had gone missing.

I was perfectly free in my seven-year-old body and in communion with the land. That property was my version of heaven. An old barn tilted sideways at the end of the gravel drive, with a fantastic looming silo crumbling behind it. Further back, a large field rolled up to a gentle creek and a smattering of Maple and Oak trees, chittering squirrels and belly-bulging bullfrogs every which way.

With widespread yards on either side of a white, peeling-paint house, our home was a perpetual playground. Bicycles leaned against each other at the house's edge with rusted chains and well-worn handles from hours of gripping. A volleyball net and a variety of sport balls, alongside a decorated statue of the Virgin Mary, adorned one of the yards. Chickadees, Starlings, and Woodpeckers swept in and out of the small fruit trees my father planted for my mom every Mother's Day. A crab apple tree released her fruit each fall at the top of crumbling stone steps that led to the creaky red front door.

Inside, there was no television or Internet. The phone, corded in the kitchen, was a rotary dial; if anyone called, privacy was never assumed. The dining room held an enormous table surrounded by chairs, pressed against each other so that every elbow at dinner touched. All us kids would argue who got to sit next to Mom at dinnertime, sometimes beginning at the first sign of daylight: "Can I sit next to you tonight, Mom?" Fights regularly ensued between us as we tried to corner Mom early. After dinner chores were complete, multiple couches, beds, and cushions offered hubs for our butts as we consumed book after book from the local library. A crackling wood stove sat center in the living room, a hub for countless games like checkers, chess, gin rummy, and Scrabble.

By that stove we huddled in the wintertime and gathered for family meetings and prayer. A crucifix hung in most rooms, a reminder to us that Jesus suffered and died for our salvation. Our parents were fiercely Catholic and nary a moment went by without the reminder that Jesus (or some holy saint) was watching us. Pope John Paul II kept a watchful eye from his portrait on the wall — the kind who's eyes followed you wherever you stood — and votive candles burned regularly next to a Bible.

Many Sunday nights, my parents would host prayer gatherings with other Catholic families, called a Cenacle. These are faith-sharing groups, named after the room where Jesus had his last supper with his disciples before he was crucified. Each one lasted for a few hours — an eternity to a child. I loved having so many people around me, but I hated how still and quiet I had to be. Each gathering was filled with recitations of the rosary and the Divine Mercy Chaplet, as well as songs like "Michael

Row the Boat A-shore, Hallelujah." I remember wearing my Sunday poofy dresses and making sure my legs were covered while I sat on the floor with my other siblings, reciting prayers with duty. The reward for honoring our parents' religion would be trays of brownies and desserts, and a full out sprint in the backyard with squirt guns or a rallying game of Calvin Ball (for all the Calvin and Hobbes fans out there).

Our home was a bubble. We were protected from the world without a TV telling us the news or the internet giving us never-ending access to stories. Attending private Catholic schools in the next town over, we listened to whatever Mom would let us turn on via the radio on the way to the stoic brick building of Mater Dolorosa (Latin for "sorrowful mother," the depiction of Jesus' mother as he dies on the cross). Dad would take us out of school only for things like pilgrimages to day-long services at Church on holy days. Catholicism was our main connection to a world bigger than the farmland. It was the biggest channel of life that I knew as a child.

But, like I said: the farm home I grew up in was heaven to me. What I had access to seemed to surpass in importance anything I was reciting in my Cenacles or at Church or in school: Nature. My dirt-caked fingertips could touch everything I personally felt to be close-to-God on our farm property.

I spent hours in the back field looking for bugs and beetles of all kinds. With my siblings, we foraged for wild berries, and slept under the stars at a campsite by the creek beyond the back field. We captured frogs and released them in new places as a generous hope for their survival. In the wintertime, we trekked into the nearby golf course, sledding down the massive hill behind the clubhouse and stomping holes into the ice by the snow-covered green way.

Everything felt like a zone of discovery. We were making up stories of all the creatures we found and unearthing new sensory experiences with every day-long adventure into the back woods. The cool black earth pressed between my toes; water bugs slid past leaping frogs midst a crinkling tinkle of creek; sweet juice from a strand of grass dribbled down my chin as I chewed, mimicking a farmer I once saw in a book illustration; birdsong and wind through old oak tree branches composed background music I could swirl round and round to.

I don't remember the feeling of boredom; but I remember the long loping day unfolding in front of us with nothing planned to do. It prompted us to create, to play pretend, to curate our own entertainment. We made our way through the '90s and early 2000s atop the trees we climbed, on trips to the local library by bike, and inside of blanket forts with entire story lines attached to our play. And gritting our teeth through community prayer time.

My brother Joe, was an exceptional story creator. He could take a simple moment of quiet and transform it into something new and exciting. I adored him for that. We could be World War II pilots one afternoon, and the next, characters from *The Canterbury Tales*, on a long and dusty pilgrimage. He went on to become a priest, lacing his homilies with story, detail, and delight to capture the love of his congregation.

Joe caught the storytelling bug from my father. On special occasions, Dad would put us all to bed instead of my mother, standing in the landing that separated the boys' room from the girls'. The girls' room — two bunk beds and a baby bed — held five of us at one time. The boys' room had a single bunk bed with just the two boys, Joe and Sam. There was no door on the girls' room; instead, it had a sheet tacked to the frame for privacy.

So Dad stood there, between the two rooms, and laced story after story for us. Between Joe and my father, I fell in love with the richness of tales. Dad would tell stories about the raccoon he saved from a trap in his late teens and sing songs like "You Can't Get to Heaven on Roller skates." (I really had a hard time believing that one, but it was a catchy song.)

More than the storytelling and imaginative games, my childhood was filled with long summers in my favorite tree, scribbling poems into notebooks and making long lists of things I wanted to do:

- Catch frogs
- Ride my bike to the library
- Roll down the big hill at the golf course
- Make a castle in the sand pile beneath the tree house
- Make dandelion jewelry for mom
- Climb trees and spy on the neighbors
- Create a mud pie picnic
- Read enough books to get a Book It pizza
- Walk to the blueberry patches

The slow, daily life of the farm was a prompt to thumb through my list, pick what sounded good and right to me — and just do it.

I was unbounded and alive. My hair was free and my stomach bare as I tore through the garden as a shirtless toddler, arms up as I balanced my teetering. Wild berry stained my fingertips, and little red scratches appeared on my skin from hugging the new kittens too tightly. Sunshine dripped into my pores like butter on the corn cob I had wrestled with during dinner on the lawn.

My little girl self thrived. She was alive. She was just about to get orders from the religious world of what a woman is "supposed" to be and of how ladylike she needed to act in order to be valued. But at that time, she was simply attuned to the world around her. The landscape was precious, offering her a home to be a child within. The freest version of myself, this child, was in communion with nature: wild and free.

Sometimes, when I close my eyes, I can still feel her: barefoot, breathless with delight, chasing frogs across the field.

Two and a half decades later, I remembered her as I sat in my small house, nestled into a different dead-end street, but now in South Minneapolis as an adult. Nary a crucifix in sight; instead, a candle burned by a deck of tarot cards and a small collection of crystals. I was sipping coffee on a mid-century couch my partner Chris and I found on Facebook Marketplace for half its worth in the middle of the pandemic. In front of me was sprawled my journal and favorite pen — inky and black a

19

with a good weight to it. My dog, Blue the boxer, was curled at my side. An enormous TV sat black across from me, and the low-level hum of constant power, surging through cords, WiFi, and screens, buzzed around me. No longer in that home on a dead end street in Western Massachusetts, but remembering the little girl who did.

Thirty years old and I was reminiscing on that version of little me. I looked down at my journal, flopped open to line after line of inky curiosity. I'd just written on the page:

> *How did that carefree child learn that her body was anything other than incredible, an instrument to feel and be in the world? Could something like training for a 100-mile race help me return to her brilliance? What new story do I want to tell myself? Tell others? How had I lost touch with her over the years — that little girl, so wild and free?*

I was now well into adulthood and experiencing a reckoning with my body. There was a pile-up of old beliefs I accrued over the years that prompted me to lose touch with a simple, empowering part of myself; a part that was beginning to stir in me again, asking me to come out and play. And as a runner, I felt I had a pretty dependable thread back to myself. I could take my body onto the trails and allow myself to reconnect with the churn of my legs that the little girl in me once knew so well.

There in Minneapolis, decades away from the child I once was, something sparked inside of me. I wanted to nose dive into personal discovery and was willing to look back into my timeline to unearth my story. I was willing to see where it would all take me.

What follows on these pages is the woven story of who this little girl was, how her body and mind were impacted as a child and late teen, and what ultimately carried her onto the trails of the Leadville Trail 100 Run in Colorado. It's a story about her body, and what that body both carried and shed on her way through this iconic race. It's a story about breaking down internal barriers created by institutions and expectations. It's also a story about personal empowerment, forgiveness, and healing.

In my journal that day in Minneapolis, the thirty-year old was ready for something bigger than herself.

Standing at the edge of something new, the thirty-year old knew that her little girl wildness would come whispering back soon enough. It was just a matter of when, and how.

A story meant to unfold.

4

1995

Hopped a pogo stick
for hours.
Bathing suits in
April showers.
Chestnuts dipped
With melted butter.
Read a book in
laundry's clutter.
Family forts
stretched out sheets.
Evenings spent there
underneath.
Played checkers chess
on dad's belly.
Paper sacks
peanut butter jelly.
Barn cats swatted
at the swallows.
Bedtimes built

for tomorrow.
Gravel crunch:
mom's finally home.
Count on one hand
the days alone.
Broccoli, chicken
pasta, repeat.
Cereal, eggs
garden kale to eat.
Heads up seven up
Marco polo.
Traded a slinky
for a shiny yo-yo.
Clanging bell
time for dinner.
Cracked red deck
guaranteed a splinter.
High waist grass
in the fields.
Pulled out ticks
to shrieks and squeals.
Walked to the corner
bought a pop.
Rode our bikes
easy free nonstop.
Spun round and round
to get real dizzy.
Uncle and Dad
sipping whiskey.
Pulled out stray weeds
on a Saturday.

Invited neighbors
out to play —
In '95 I didn't
once consider:
Nostalgia tastes both
sweet and bitter.

5

I'm Sorry, I Love You

Twenty-seven years before Race Day

I did not like this. Not one bit.

At barely six years old, I fought to keep the tears from my eyes. My mother's hand was nestled in mine as we walked lightly through the tall, unmowed grass in our side yard. We were barefoot, the loose linen of our dresses slipping around our calves in the summer breeze. Dragonflies and butterflies flitted en route to sunny landing places — the wild rose bush by the woodshed and the sea of dandelions beyond it. A bee buzzed much too closely to us. A breath caught in my throat and I gasped involuntarily at the bee, burying my face in my mother's legs.

"It's okay," my mother softly nudged as I gripped her thighs. "Say, 'I love you, bees. I'm sorry, bees.' "

The haven of her skirted legs was appealing, safe. The bees

were not.

I felt her hand press against the blonde of my head, and she swooped my hair through her fingers — a gentle prompt. I peered out nervously to look for the bees before retreating back into the fabric tussle.

"I love you, bees," I whispered into her body.

Turning and crouching down, she met me at eye level, rubbing my back with affection. I was safe now; I was okay. The bees weren't here to harm me — especially if I wasn't harming them.

Two days earlier, I had been swarmed by a throb of them, my bare summer skin lit up by their stinging defenses. Moments before the onslaught, my brother Joe and I had been playing thoughtlessly behind the old barn at the back of our home's property. Layered piles of boards laden with nails, rotten slabs of wood, and rusted pipe littered the ground. This area was out-of-bounds according to my parents — and rightly so; yet my siblings and I never paid much attention to that rule. Play consumed us with make-believe time travel into colonial times, and we built rickety forts in the hallowed silo nearby, to my parent's chagrin.

Joe shouted some kind of call-to-action to us, like "Charge!" or maybe even, "To the summit!" I followed after him — charging, or to-ing — high knees and punching fists. Suddenly, we lost our footing. The boards beneath us gave way, and our little legs crashed through the rotted wood.

Barely a second passed before a buzzing swarm encapsulated us. I was blinded by the fury, buzzing and stinging and a cloud of shimmering insect bodies all around me. Red raged across my eyes, and through the throb of noise, I could hear screaming. *Who is screaming?* I remember thinking. It was me.

A door slammed beyond the barn and a determined crunch of footsteps rained closer toward us. Both Joe and I were in a mess of bees, sting after sting on our tiny bodies. I was lost in a black daze that arrived with extreme pain — and then, the shock of nothingness. It could have been a lifetime or seconds, but I felt myself lifted off the ground, pulled into a familiar armpit. My father. Sweeping mounds of bees from my skin, he somehow transported both of us from the back of the barn into the house. Suddenly I felt ice-cold water, as sudden as the stings. I gasped as Dad plunged me into the bathtub.

I'm sure my father took us from the ice bath to the hospital and I'm sure it was stressful. Both Joe and I were safe and cared for in the end. I got a Pink Panther ice cream pop and delighted in the hard candy nose that turned into gum. That day, my father was my hero. I thought he'd always hold me tight and scoop bees off my skin, lessening pain as much as he could in my life.

Unfortunately, I found my father emotionally unpredictable in my childhood — a complicated explosion of uncertainty. He was hardworking: laboring in the garden on the weekends and full days at the local jail during the week. He was creative: building furniture for my mother, planting beautiful trees with the seasons, and tuning the harmonica to our giggling whims. But he also seemed tired and easily angered. He had little patience for too-loud giggles and the constant whir of chatter that came from a house with twelve children. All too many happy, innocent moments were broken by the whiplash of his emotions.

Spanking, as for many in the nineties, was a formality in our home. If we misbehaved, if we got too loud, if we were too much — we got a spanking.

It was as normal as breakfast or brushing our teeth. First, we'd do something that was tagged as naughty. Then, we were ushered to the stairs, which was a commonplace spot in the home for a public rump slap. My father would pull our pants down, exposing our bare butts to the audience of siblings who, no doubt, were "learning their lesson," and slap us — hard and loud. Red marks from the wedding ring on his left hand accompanied my skin. Commonplace as it was, I know many of us have a version this spanking story. I believe my parents did the best they could with the information they had, using force as a means to parent well. But of course — it hurt. And the hurt lingered long after the red hand prints faded from our skin.

A social worker by education, Dad had a good friend whom we affectionately called Uncle. One day, Uncle informed my father that he should use a belt instead of hand-spanking. If so, Uncle reasoned, the child would associate the punishment with the tool instead of the parent — protecting the relationship of father and child.

It was Saturday afternoon nap time; we were supposed to be snoozing. The box fans in each room were whirring, sending lazy hot air around the otherwise stagnant room.

Instead of choosing sleep, my siblings and I opted to dash in a frenzied game of tag. My mom was probably nursing one of my baby sisters in her bedroom, my dad most likely out in the garden working. A false sense of freedom empowered us.

Like an indoor track, the top floor of our farm house was set up so that one could run down the hall, zip through the girls' bedroom with the two bunk beds, through the open doorway to the adjoining laundry room, and ricochet out that doorway to the top of the stairs — ready to sprint around all over again.

(In later years, I would be an avid indoor track athlete and participate in many joyful, excited loops inside — no spanking interruptions telling me to stop, just the bell at the final lap telling me to GO AND GO NOW.)

Zooming around inside, though, was classic naughty behavior for all of us. Even naughtier when my father walked into the house — beaten by the sun and weary from the full week behind him of working with inmates at the Correctional Center. We were blissfully unaware of his entrance as we ran, screamed, and made happy noises.

Before I knew what was happening, red rage engulfed the room. This time, my father wasn't there to save me; this time, he was the danger. He had his belt clamped in hand and wasted no time hitting it against my backside. Without any warning, I was whipped.

Unsurprisingly, I was confused. Was my father there to protect and care for me, like he did with the bees? Or was he the one I needed protection from? Why did I want to spend the early mornings with him on his fishing trips or planting with him on the garden, hoping to feel special in his presence, while there were welts still freshly healing on my bottom?

Our parents, imperfect in their humanity, bring us into the world and care for us to the best of their ability. The very thing our parents wanted as children, they might be incapable of creating fully with their own. As an adult with a widened lens, I have compassion for my parents: we only have access to the tools we have access to. At the time, Dad's best tool was this punishment.

However, as a six year-old, there was no way I could grasp a nuanced concept of tough love.

Then there was the way my mom got good at explaining away my father's behavior: "He was once hit by a car," she'd explain. "He's quick to anger. Be good and he won't get provoked."

I can understand the intention of love there— knowing my mother loves my father fiercely. And I respect that. But what did I learn from those moments of punishment? What was the lasting impression of him that followed me into adulthood? To this day, I have an automatic stress response to someone coming through the door unannounced or unexpectedly. I jump at sudden loud noises. And, I got involved in relationships that had a touch of control woven throughout them.

I think part of it is that some men can get absolution for their bad behavior — for unregulated emotions and for being at fault. What I ended up learning at a young age was that men can get the write-offs and excuses and *oh-pardon-him* — and little girls, when they aren't good or following the rules or being nice and quiet and sweet... little girls get punished. (My brothers were certainly not immune to any of this; yet, I cannot speak on their behalf.)

Thus began my complicated (and tiresome) understanding that the man who could protect me and love me could also harm me; that it was imperative to be a "good girl" to be loved — to be worthy. I had to be the one to say, *I love you. I'm sorry.* I carried this understanding in my heart; it kept me safe in my body as a child and, naturally, it followed me throughout my life. I carried this understanding into my relationship with myself and relationships with men.

I wanted to be worthy, to be special, to be seen. I wanted to be wild and free, but I also wanted to do right in my father's eyes.

And so, when my dad took up running, I did, too.

6

I Run Because It's Me

The air was cool and dry. My bare feet hit the soft dirt behind our house, dust kicking up behind me as my arms were wildly with no rhythm, no technique — just joy. There wasn't really a goal. There definitely weren't any stopwatches. It was just me, my siblings, and our pretend races around the back field. Evelyn would start us off with a dramatic "GO!" Sarah would giggle before taking off in the wrong direction, arms flailing, her hair streaming behind her. Joe thumped the ground with his dirt-caked bare feet, racing me shoulder to shoulder.

I ran because it felt good, because as a little girl it felt like flying.

Something clicked in me when I moved like that. I didn't have words for it then, but my legs and my heart knew. Running made me feel important. Not in a loud way, not in the way that demanded attention — but in a quiet, rooted, deeply personal way. The world made more sense when I was in motion.

I wasn't thinking about being ladylike. I wasn't thinking about behaving or fitting a perfect definition of a good Catholic girl. I wasn't thinking about being small or quiet to stay out of Dad's way, but of just being alive.

Truthfully, running was the first thing that ever felt like *mine.* Even though my dad was the one to first take me onto the trails and run with me, it was as though I got a gift that was mine to unwrap and play with as I liked. I could stretch my legs and fly; I could pound the ground as I pleased, the earth pressing back with soft laughter. I could leave the press of Catholicism and run outside anytime I wanted to, anyway I desired — as long as it was after Church.

By high school, that love had shape and it had structure. We got uniforms. There were whistles and track workouts and time trials. There were busses to away races at neighboring schools and finish lines with the occasional reporter. I started caring about how fast I was. I started noticing who was watching. And somewhere along the way, I started getting *good.*

I remember one of my first cross country races vividly — the crack of the gun, the churn of feet beside me, the fluttering nerves that turned to fire once I started moving. I remember the cool breeze against my face, the smell of fall leaves, the burn in my lungs as I pushed toward a finish line that suddenly *mattered. I suddenly mattered.*

That race was the first time I noticed grown-ups clapping for me: specifically, parents of my teammates and my coach. I mean really clapping — their eyes on *me,* their hands coming together with what felt like genuine pride. And in that moment,

I felt seen in a way that didn't require being quiet or small.

My coach was a man named Mr. Goda and he paid attention. He noticed effort and spirit. And he believed in me. He encouraged the way I ran — told me I was strong and that I had grit. He offered correction without shame, praise without expectation. There was no emotional whiplash with him. Just steadiness. Support. Encouragement. When I couldn't afford a pair of racing spikes for the upcoming season, he brought me to a local run shop to purchase my first pair.

I remember one practice freshman year when I showed up late, my cheeks burning with embarrassment, expecting to be scolded. He just smiled and said, "Go warm up." That was it. No lecture. No punishment. Just grace and the push to go do hard work.

It sounds small — and maybe it was — but to a young girl learning how to navigate approval and fear, the rules of being liked or loved, that kind of grace left a mark. It was a positive, lasting mark on me of what healthy masculine energy can feel like.

I loved running. I loved the way it let me feel powerful in my body, the way it connected me to my sisters, and to a version of myself that didn't have to apologize for being loud or fast or fierce. And I loved having someone in my corner who saw me not for how good I was at being small — but for how strong I was when I took up space.

Now when I run I carry her with me — the girl who sprinted

through the back fields of Western Mass with berry-stained fingers and wind-whipped hair. I carry the teenager who showed up to practice, ready to push herself, to feel her heart pound in her chest and know it meant she was alive.

And, I carry the woman who still believes that when we run — when we move forward with our full selves — we become something braver, bolder, freer. No matter our gender, our belief systems, or our creeds.

Running found me long, long before I found Leadville.

7

Birthright

I don't believe in
a God
a Universe
an Energy
who created
all of me
including
my bare-breasted vibrancy
who somehow
prefers
I stay still
keep small
and just
behave.

8

Meeting God

Thirty years before Race Day

"Barbara," the voice boomed.

I froze, mid-wail, my chubby baby cheeks wet with misery at being left alone to go to sleep.

"Barbara; this is God."

This was my first memory — of God or anything else for that matter. I was barely three years old.

I was born midweek in autumn to six siblings awaiting my arrival while they sat begrudgingly at school desks. My mother had already birthed four boys and two girls when I made my entrance into the world. I was lucky number seven.

Just over a year old, I developed a raised bump beneath and to the middle side of one of my eyes, at the bridge of my button nose. It was red with blue veins pulsing beneath it, like an enormous bug bite. It wasn't apparent what it was at first take. My parents did what they could, taking me to specialists in Boston — a ninety minute drive from our home. I'm sure an early sense of patience was born in me as I got strapped into my booster seat and soared off down the highway toward another specialist, another appointment, the minutes trickling by. Perhaps it was then that I felt special, and wanted to remain so.

It resulted in a harmless mass of blood, an inflamed area that would dissipate over time; and, in time, it did. I can hold the crinkled photographs from that season and see the evolution of baby-with-a-bump into kindergartner-with-an-adorably-clear-face.

During the unknown period of that bump, my parents, the ever avid Catholics, prayed over me. Got me blessed by priests. Wiped holy oils over my troubled face. I believe I was given a special kind of attention during those early years — an attention my body would crave, ask for, in the many years to follow.

Like there, in the crib, as a toddler.

I was alone; and didn't understand why. I needed to be held, to be loved, to have lips pressed against my cheeks, the warm heartbeat of a chest I could lean into. I'm not sure why I awoke or what prompted me awake. I simply remember that I was alone in a crib, light piercing through the crack in the bedroom door, and someone named God was outside it talking to me.

"Barbara, no more crying," the voice vibrated in my little chest.

Just as I sniffled enough oxygen to fuel the next bout of tears, the voice boomed again:

"Barbara, this is God. No more crying. Go to sleep."

God.

I hadn't met him yet. This was a big deal.

My parents talked to me about this man. The man who was all-knowing and who knew when we were naughty. The man who had a son who died for all of us to live. The man who called the shots, who knew what was right, and what was wrong. The man in charge.

If God was here, speaking to me, I had to listen. I just had to!

The tears settled as I choked the naughtiness back inside of me.

"Good girl. Go to sleep."

It didn't fully occur to me until junior high that I could question this world I was given. It was science class. I sat in the back row, thirteen and full of finger-flicking push back. I had electric blue pumps on my feet and was chipping away at illegal-to-school nail polish on each hand. Sister Someone was at the front, donned in her gray habit, and telling the story of Creation, or the adventurous trip of Moses, or the shuffling that Noah had to do to get the animals on the ark. Whatever the story was, I didn't like it. And so, my teenage brain tested out how to share that.

"Ughhhh," a long, exasperated sigh left my lips, and I could feel the teenage exasperation roll down my throat into the pit of my stomach to live there.

The room fell silent. Eyes turned to me, and Sister's small frame somehow rose tall at the front.

"Do you have something to say, Miss Powell?" She knew me by now. I liked to wear bright makeup, even though it wasn't permitted at Catholic school. I rolled up my skirt and wasn't afraid of a little sass now and then.

I avoided eye contact, staring down at my chipped nails. Something must have made its way out of my mouth — some kind of comment that Bible stories didn't seem as true as she made them out to be. Whatever I said, it was naughty. I was back in that crib. I was back on the stairs, waiting for a spanking — God, or one of his spokespeople, had to step in. I was out of line.

Sister ordered me to the principal's office. When ushered in, I plopped in front of another nun, higher up in power, and was told through squinted eyes:

"Why can't you be more like your sister?" It was a pointed accusation, chastising me for the unruliness I created instead of sitting still and behaving. My two older sisters, Evelyn and Mary, had already graduated with respect from the nuns. I didn't seem to match up.

As my brain formed just enough to detect an identity — to shape opinions, thoughts, and ideas — I found rebellion. Like all teenagers do.

I repelled anything Catholic-related during this time. In my teenage years, I abhorred the Church—resenting any of its teachings. I rejected the strict path it laid out for me, as I didn't accept a God who disallowed space to ask questions, or the freedom to cry when I was in pain, or the thrill of running with wild abandon.

This version of God was imprinted in me — quieting me, pressing me to acquiesce, to follow the rules and *just go to sleep.* A voice of control and a guidance away from the most feminine, charged, powerful parts of myself.

But what about a God who delighted in my wild ways? Who celebrated my thighs, my wailing, my darkest parts? Who rejoiced in my competitive thrills and my ever-sideways, inquisitive brain?

I would wrestle with my relationship with the divine over the years. When one is pressed underwater, mouth agape and unable to breathe, yet told the water is safe and necessary to live a good life — to just give in — one can let go or fight it.

Many of us are told what God is, or isn't. However, many of us might never question it.

I, on the other hand, have been questioning since that moment in the crib.

Over the years, I've updated what I believe God to be. My version of God doesn't emerge from a power dynamic. It doesn't live in organized religion or an ancient script. There's no shame storm that my version ignites — no pressing feeling of "less than" or subservience.

My version of God would slowly rise from the trails that I ran on. In the kindness of coaches who supported me. In the teammates who partnered with me. In the winding wood paths, trees bowing in reverence to the majesty of the wind. In the throb of both pleasure and pain in my body.

My version of God doesn't have a specific container for me to live in — to operate from. My version of God is quite female. Intuitive. Supportive. Compassionate. Healing and alive in all the world around me. She was listening but not directive.

I'd meet my version of God out on the Colorado trails, over thirty years later. She would later follow me everywhere on the trails of the Leadville 100. She'd keep me safe and send me support when I needed it. She'd whisper in my ear, *I love you* — no apologies necessary.

I'd feel what it meant to be buoyant and free.

I realize now: the water is so expansive, so clear, and so blissful — I only had to float, to go with *Her* flow. No longer would I be held under tow, unable to breathe. And then, when I was ready to float, I was ready to say yes to bigger, brighter dreams for me. But floating did not come easy at first.

I had to wrangle a few earth-bound relationships before I could make room for my version of God and find Leadville at just the right time.

9

Never Again

Five years before Race Day

I hadn't an ounce of personal power within me. Or so it felt.

I was standing inside an apartment door in a suburb north of the Twin Cities, trying to open the door out to the hallway. A man's body towered over me — six feet plus, and every inch of it packed with muscle — his two hands holding the door shut.

"Let me out."

My voice was sturdy but flickered, like a blue flame powering it from the inside. My legs were strong from marathon training and Cross Fit, but my will was starting to fade — a weakened wilt.

He pressed the door with a large, flat hand, refusal in his eyes, but not saying a word. My eyes filled with tears, pissing me off even more.

Was that triumph on his face?

He began to coo, "Let's talk," in a much-too-soft, untrustwor-thy kind of way. This striking yet toxic man was my current boyfriend. We'd been together for a few months, a relationship I sought out after a broken engagement to someone else. I was so desperate for love and affection, that I ignored many of the so-called red flags up to this point.

The flame inside me sputtered — slowly enlarged by the oxygen in the room.

"Let me out. NOW," I began to raise my voice.

I attempted to push him away from me and the door, ten fingers palming against an iron chest. It was in vain; his body was too strong, too big, to grant me access out the door.

I was trapped.

"God damn it," I said, all breath and barely words, crumpling to the ground in defeat.

My body thrust me back in time — to the quiet farmhouse in Western Massachusetts. My heartbeat quickened as my psyche remembered: I had felt bound there, too. Bound to the house on a dead-end street. Bound to a patriarchal religion, my voice seemingly powerless. I could shout, I could scream — but as a child, it would only warrant a spanking, a verbal warning, and/or confinement in my bedroom.

Anger was a suppressed emotion to us girls in my home. It was not to be accessed, unless you were my father; if it was, it was a punishable offense. Unruly for a young lady. Disrespectful.

There, defeated and down in that northern Minneapolis apartment, a thought occurred to me: I was physically reliving something from my childhood. Not completely, but remnants.

A thought immediately buzzed into my mind: I was now an adult. I could do something different *right now*.

It was like realizing you were in the middle of a lucid dream: *I can change how this goes.*

I came back to the room from a haze of disassociation. The redheaded man was moving away from the door, sensing victory. I held the overnight bag I had brought close to my chest, my mind working as I kept my gaze downward — compliant. He softened, extending his hand to help me back up and into his arms.

Not happening.

In one swift motion, I pulled myself up by the doorknob, twisted it, thrust the door open, and ran down the hall toward the stairs. I got into my car, locking it as soon as the door swung shut.

As I drove away, I vowed: This was it. There was no safe love in his presence. There was only possession and control. The few months we spent together was more than enough to see this.

This was not the woman I was meant to be. My thoughts drifted in the car as I drove away, remembering what happened just the week before this moment.

The redhead and I were at the State Fair, enjoying ourselves. The warm day had turned into a sparkling night. Sipping beers and eating fried food, we wandered playfully from bovine exhibits to amusement games and shopping stalls.

As we exited the fairgrounds late that night, he began to show signs of drunk aggression toward me. He argued with heat, pressing about something, forcing the attention of others our way. No matter what I said or did, it seemed to stoke his fury further. He stomped. He yelled. It reached a nasty high and I felt exposed — as though his biting words were stripping me of my self-respect, word by word. This wasn't like our normal spats; this was bordering on dangerous.

Boarding the shuttle back to his neighborhood, I had had enough.

I refused to sit with him.

That really set him off.

On the shuttle, in front of a crowd of glassy-eyed, well-fed Midwestern fair goers, he harassed me from his seat across the bus. I leaned my forehead into the window glass, doing my best to ignore him.

He continued. Relentless.

Finally, a man sitting next to me in the aisle seat stiffened, sitting up tall — as though to help block me, as nonchalantly as possible. He did not budge, nor do I remember him saying anything, but he stayed firm beside me as I tried to disappear.

When the shuttle pulled up to our stop, I got up, excusing myself and flashing an apology with my eyes at the others. Like so many women before me, I felt the weight of responsibility for *his* behavior — as though I had to be the one to smooth out how everyone on that bus felt. I calmly walked past them, a tight-lipped smile the best I could offer.

Once on the pavement, I walked ahead, my phone out and the Uber app pulled up. The redhead began to plead for me to stay with him.

"No."

I was firm.

Again, red rage from him.

He grabbed my arm, but I pulled away. The night blurred as I stood my ground, waiting for the Uber to arrive, darting from his grasp every time he tried to grab me.

Someone saw his behavior— a young man on a bicycle who happened to be passing by. A small but mighty gift from the universe.

He became my voice, amplifying everything I was saying,

positioning himself between us, just like the man on the shuttle — but more vocal about it.

"She doesn't want to go with you, man. Leave her alone, dude. Walk away."

And then, turning toward me with gentle eyes, he said, "Are you okay? Do you need a ride? Can I help?"

The Uber pulled up. The young man on the bike guarded me as I got in, shaking, and the tears finally released. The driver was an older gentleman, Indian, my father's age. He watched me in the rear view mirror, concerned:

"Do you have someone you can call? I'll make sure you get inside okay. Here's my card. Please let me know if you need anything."

Once inside my apartment, I was suffocated with distress.

How could I let myself get here?

How could I allow someone to treat me like this — how could I not see all the red flags, the signs? Didn't I know better?

Red-faced, I was pissed — but I was also scared that I had been too brazen in my dismissal of the redhead, that I had upset *him* in the process of leaving. In the flurry of confusing emotions, I attempted to sleep.

The next morning, I awoke to a barrage of texts and missed

calls.

I opened the window, let the birdsong roll in, and poured steaming coffee into a mug that said *You Are Gorgeous.* But I felt ugly. Needy. The rise of shame is a muddy thing.

I agreed to see him again, the night I finally pushed the door open and ran away. I was hoping an apology would rinse me clean. I was hoping that he would understand how he hurt me and how endangered I felt.

It was too big a hope for him to fulfill.

Instead, he told me that *I* had an anger problem.

It was a bullet meant to disarm me. A comment, I believe, meant to trick me into thinking that standing up for myself — standing firm in what I wanted, creating boundaries — was wrong. Misplaced. A comment meant to gaslight.

What was I experiencing?

Yes: anger.

Justified anger.

Anger that needed a voice to express itself. Anger to run out the door. Anger to leave that pattern of men I begged to love me in tender, thoughtful ways, *in spite* of their emotional outbursts. Anger that allowed me to stand my ground, to know this type of love was not okay — it was malnourished.

Anger to leave.

After the night I left his apartment (mentioned earlier in the chapter), he arrived unannounced to my home, banging on the door.

"I still have your extra car key," he spit through the keyhole. "It would be a shame if something happened to your vehicle."

All ten toes on the ground, I told him to leave. Repeatedly.

In time, he did.

I called my friend Hallie — a social worker, as reliable and steady as they come. A woman with good resources, a bright smile, and a no-bullshit attitude when needed. She went to his apartment, picked up my things, and told him — in her own way — to fuck off.

That evening, I went out to a nearby lake and ran.

I ran until the tears finally flowed, until something dislodged in my throat.

Craning my neck toward the sky, I let out a rasping growl of a groan — as if gargling gravel.

I ran past the weeping willows that kissed the edge of the water and wished to live in their trunks like a woodland critter. I ran straight through groups of honking geese and shallow puddles. I ran on sidewalks and down the middle of the street, through unevenly mowed fields and by playgrounds — chaotic. My chest heaved and I swallowed as much oxygen as I could muster, sputtering as I went.

I am never going to be in such an unstable, awful relationship ever again, I thought.

I had the people I needed in my life, the direction I wanted to go in — and no man was going to disrupt that flow for me. Not ever again. I would see to it.

Right?

I had a hard time believing myself.

My body trembled — a strange mix of living in raw power and moving on the cusp of collapse. I ran, alone. I listened to my feet slap the pavement. I watched the sun slip into the cool sheets of the horizon as the moon cradled her way into the charcoal sky. The miles melted into a number I've long forgotten at a pace per mile that never mattered.

But my legs, my heart, my lungs — they all remember what running has done for me. Running lets me go home to my body. Running feels like a safety net in a world of uncertainty. Running is how I remind my body that she is in charge.

She is always in charge.

That night, I knew I was coming into my power — but I was still an embryo, not yet fully formed. However, I knew: I was going to rise from the shards of a broken pattern and learn what love really meant to me — what safe, stable, good love truly felt like.

And running was going to help me do it.

10

The 4 a.m. Shotgun

The starting line of the Leadville 100, Mid-August 2023

I slipped from one dream world to the next.

In the black of night, up at 10,000 feet altitude in a motel in Leadville, I slept on the edge of waking — a cliff side into the unknown of tomorrow.

The motel bed's thick quilt cocooned me, more cotton than my hot-blooded body needed. I rubbed my feet together, grasshopper-soothing I picked up from my mother. A swirl of runners melted together around me — a kaleidoscope of Nike and Brooks and Salomon shoes, running. What were they doing? Where were they going? Why wasn't I moving, too? Looking down, I realized: no shoes of my own. I was stuck in mud, the black sucking me in place. What was happening? I needed to go. It was time to go but I couldn't move. I was stuck...

The alarm on my phone tinkled to life. It was 2:30 a.m.

My eyes eased open, consciousness registering the sound. Shapes of the motel room slowly formed, slits of streetlight stabbing sharp corners and soft edges.

Race day.

Chris groaned softly beside me, rolling to the opposite side, his head of curls bouncing as they settled back into the bed.

It was the early morning hours of the Leadville 100. My gear was laid out on a table I couldn't yet see in the darkness. The bottles I'd drink from within hours sat plump in the mini fridge.

I blinked, prompting the film to shift from my eyes. Five months of training and living at altitude. The mountain storms I got caught in. The people I met. The trails I ventured through. And the meaning — oh, the meaning! — I had made of this whole thing.

At once, I rose and shuffled toward the lamp across the motel room to switch it on.

Plink. A soft glow. The day had started.

I began to boil a pot of water for coffee and slipped over to Chris, kissing him on the cheek as he labored to breathe. A Midwestern boy, this bout at altitude was already a slight strain for him. My heart surged knowing that he was there for me, labored breath and all.

55

On the bedside table: a stack of cards and notes from my family. I took time to hold each one and reread the *Good lucks* and *We love yous.*

The water clicked off on the boiler. I poured a steaming mugful of instant coffee — 2:50 a.m.

The clothing I'd laid out the night before somehow found its way onto my body. I filled my race pack with everything I needed:

- Two water bottles with liquid fuel.
- Gels and Glukose packets.
- Cold water with hydration powder pre-mixed in the bladder.
- A small baggie with toilet paper and disposable wipes.
- Salt chews.
- My phone and headphones.
- Rain jacket.

The pack fattened with every additional item, adding weight — but I'd practiced this. I'd run all summer with a stuffed pack, learning what it meant to carry what I needed through miles of Colorado trails.

Once I'd eaten — a carb- and protein-packed breakfast bar and a coconut yogurt — and moved through a series of stretches while sipping electrolytes, I hustled out the door with my just-waking, sleepy partner by my side. Chris barely sleepwalking and myself trying to contain the energy bubbling up inside of me. We were off to the starting line — 3:35 a.m.

The sky was clear. The air, electric. My skin seemed to shimmer.

"It's here!" Giddy, I squeezed Chris's hand as we walked toward the corner of 6th and Harrison, past darkened shops and homes resting before dawn.

The start line corral was packed with people. Headlamps darted back and forth as their owners swept their heads to see: tie this shoelace, high-five or hug that person, tighten the hydration pack, move nutrition from this pocket to that one. I kept my light off to save battery and lifted my chin upward.

The sky was aglitter. It was 3:56 a.m.

Words spoken into a mic from the race director and founders. Encouragement: guts, grit, and determination. A haze of speech. Then, the national anthem. Hats pulled from heads. Hands pressed against chests. Keeping my eyes on the sky, I gasped — a shooting star streaked the night, just as "and the rockets' red glare, the bombs bursting in air" played overhead.

I turned to a man next to me. He silently nodded with a smile, acknowledging he saw the star, too.

A good omen, I thought. *I'm going to finish this thing. There is no other answer. No other way. No other outcome.*

Then, a shotgun rose to the satin sky. In seconds, it charged, bellowing into the wispy morning. It was finally 4:00 a.m.

We began to move.

I turned to see Chris and my friend Trapper (who would pace me later in the race) beaming from the sidelines.

"Go get 'em, Barbara!" Trapper punched the air with his fist. Chris mouthed the words, "I love you, honey" and I'm almost positive I felt him wink.

I swallowed the moment whole; I was on my way.

The plan was to stay relaxed and easy, settling into a pace I was almost uncomfortable with because of how slow it was. That should have meant around 12- to 13-minute miles. But the buildup of energy from a taper, and the thrill of race day, meant I started out under 10-minute miles for the first few.

Every mile alert on my watch brought my coach, Greg, to mind: *Go easy, girl. Stick to the plan.*

Greg had been a huge help getting me to the start — as were so many others.

Before race week, I'd met up with a local ultra runner, Don, for coffee and insight on what to expect. He's an exceptional distance athlete — lives full-time in Fairplay, Colorado and holds the 100-mile treadmill world record, as well as being an American champion in the 24-hour race. His demeanor is open and kind, with a natural joyfulness in his voice and body as he talks about running.

THE 4 A.M. SHOTGUN

During our meetup, Don gave me a piece of advice:

"Wear a buff or handkerchief over your nose and mouth for the first few miles," he told me.

"You'll be mid-pack and there will be a ton of dirt kicked up on the road leading out of the start line toward Turquoise Lake."

Buff pulled over my nose, I relaxed into my stride.

The crunch of footfalls and shuffle of clothing offered a soft melody to run to. Conversations and laughter wove through the darkness. Another group of runners recognized me from the Life Time Foundation, and we shared a brief, high-note exchange.

But once the first few miles slipped away, I pulled inward and tapped into a solemn, steady rhythm.

We entered the trail at Turquoise Lake — a single track. One bobbing headlamp in front of the other. The moon splashed against the water, and the alpine trees parted for our journey. With a careful eye, I watched the ground ahead and the heels of the runner before me, side-stepping roots and rocks.

I was doing the thing.

I was running this race.

I was in my body, moving step by step, away from the starting line, toward something brave and new. Nothing ahead but footsteps and sky. And everything inside of me that I needed.

11

How We Said I Love You

"I want to feel big,"
I told you
as I traced my fingers
along your skin.
My thumb caught your chin
as my eyes
slipped down
to your lips.
I stroked your left cheek
with a knuckle
and whispered,
"You make me feel big
instead of
so
small."
You brought your mouth
to mine,
kissed me
with a punctuation

I hadn't yet
encountered,
and told me,
"Take up all
the space
you need."

12

Love and Pizza

Four and a half years before Race Day

Chris entered the scene not too long after that bleak evening. Of course, he didn't know when he met me that he'd one day wake up to a 3 a.m. alarm in Leadville, Colorado, to support me as I ran 100 miles. And on the way there, he'd become my safe place to land — no matter where my explorations of the heart took me.

Like many great things, our love took its time.

Chris was once just a guy in a flannel button-down at a pizza shop, serving slices of hot pizza and pints of cold beer.

The night I met him, it was early fall, mere days after walking out on the red head and just after my 30th birthday. I was driving around Minneapolis looking for a place to eat. The red head had sent me a text an hour earlier, trying to connect with me.

Fuck that, I thought. I deleted his number and, for good measure, blocked him.

A thick book for grad school jostled on the passenger seat: *Motivational Interviewing.* Entering the final year of my master's program, I was on the cusp of becoming a board-certified health and wellness coach. After working for Nike and Skechers in the footwear industry throughout my twenties, I had pivoted. This degree gave me a route into wellness with both credibility and impact — there was good work to be done.

I had to catch up on reading, and I wanted to do it with cheese and beer.

I drove through Uptown Minneapolis, surveying my options. Across the street from my inching car was a hometown spot called Galactic Pizza. I hadn't been yet, but I'd heard good things, so I decided to drive forward until I could make a U-turn and park safely. As I clocked my path to turn, a cyclist shot out of my blind spot. Spooked, I swept my blinker off and barreled straight through the next intersection instead.

Heart pounding, I noticed a sign up ahead, neon-lit: Pizza Luce.

Well, I thought, *that'll work.*

Like a moth to light, I pulled into the lot, collected my things, and made my way inside for a table.

The hostess Ellie sat me, honoring my desire to eat outside on the patio. She was short, tattooed, and flawlessly beautiful —

black hair, deep-lined eyes, goth clothing. Seating me, she plunked a glass of water on the table with a menu and a wink.

"Chris is your server tonight. He'll be right with you."

I sank into the tall-back chair and inhaled the heavy scent of hops hanging on the pergola above me.

"Coca-Cola, tap beer, lemonade?"

I looked up to see Chris and his not-quite-hazel eyes looking at me in anticipation of my order.

I smiled.

He had an easy, friendly way about him — a Minnesotan beard hugging his chin. He had the vibe of a person who wanted to be here — not just on the patio serving slices, but on Earth, experiencing life.

I liked that. An immediate buzz surged through me — not unlike the little-kid feeling from running through a sprinkler on the first real day of hot summer.

He was cute.

I watched as he left to retrieve my drink. Dark curly hair. A few inches taller than me. Black Vans on his feet and a chain wallet. A little punk rock.

While waiting for my meal, I thumbed through my book

absentmindedly, indulging in possible flirtation. With the all-too-recent nudge from friends to *"just be single,"* it felt a little soon.

But I could feel Chris's eyes on me as he came back onto the patio, cold suds in one hand, and another table's order in the other. I pretended to read. He tended to another table before sweeping over to mine, playfully coaxing me from my grad school obligations.

He lingered to talk with me.

I loved it.

That's how the evening went: smooth, crisp, easy.

Him serving me, then loitering, creating conversation. I laughed. He asked questions and I caught him looking at me from inside the shop. I texted my friend Hallie:

My server is cute. Should I ask him out?

Her reply came swiftly: *Duh, yes!*

Wrapping up the evening, Chris dropped off my check.

I dutifully added the tip, signed it... and on the extra receipt, jotted down my phone number with an invitation to call me.

Why not? I thought.

He texted me within the hour of me leaving the restaurant.

* * *

We landed on a local music venue down the road called Icehouse for our first date later that night.

Live music, low lighting, and a packed house made it hard to talk, but we did our best. As the evening wore on, so did my mentality — and my heart.

We had a solid hour of vibrant discussion — about life, each other, our families, my schooling, his upbringing in Wisconsin. But once the music started, we fell into silence together, holding our drinks, faces forward toward the stage while listening to the band.

I got lost in my head — the swell of not being ready to date so soon.

Wrapped in thoughts — pulsing, buzzing, unrelenting in my skull — I excused myself to the bathroom. Skirting around small tables with intimate moments, the band's bass thumping, I maneuvered my way to the women's room, dampness blooming in my armpits.

Looking in the mirror, I tried to compose myself.

Breathe.

I ran my wrists beneath the cold tap water to slow my heart rate.

I don't even know this guy.

However, I was at odds with how to proceed. My mind was shutting down.

Up until that point, I had largely put men and their feelings first in my life, easily discarding my own intuition and needs to make sure my date was happy.

I'd learned to be sweet, to stay small, to say sorry before I even knew what I was apologizing for; that was how I'd been taught to survive love. As a little girl, I watched my mother and father take on traditional roles, teaching me what partnership looked like in a marriage — uneven. I watched the other women in church, teaching me what value looked like in our gender — of service to the men. I watched how the girls in my family were expected to be, teaching me how to be female — small, sweet, and most certainly agreeable.

But what was going on tonight? What did *I* want?

Overwhelmed, I decided: I was going to leave.

I pushed open the bathroom door, excused myself through the back of the crowd. Just out of Chris's sight line, I slipped out the front of the venue and into the cool September night, walking myself home.

I ghosted him.

"I'm not ready for this," I puffed the words up to the stars.

Take your time, they assured me.

I walked the few miles home, placing one steady foot in front of the other. I wasn't sure if I was going to call him or not. Even when my phone buzzed with the text, "Where did you go?"

* * *

After walking out of our first date, I had to make some sense of what happened.

Chris was nice and I was genuinely attracted to him. Unfortunately, I got uncomfortable in our quiet stillness; I got scared. I didn't trust anything — including my gut or our synergy.

So, I bolted.

I had to get away, get back to myself, step into the cool autumn night and walk through the feelings that had ignited in me.

Lucky for me, Chris was gently persistent. He waited for me to be ready to let him in. And in time, I did let him in.

Later that week, I invited him to a poetry reading. He met my friends. We went out for food, hiked out onto red sandstone, and shared black coffee on cracked sidewalk patios. He held my hand as we walked and showed up at the finish lines of races I ran.

Chris listened when I spoke, and didn't rush me to complete my thoughts. I could be loud or soft, open or closed — and he was game for it. Whatever version of myself needed to emerge, he did his best to make room for it. To make room for *me.*

In time, I slowly felt safe. Seen. In time, I felt special. Important. The little girl in me began to peek out from her hiding place. She didn't have to brace for impact. She didn't have to calculate how to be palatable. She didn't have to run. The little girl opened to the possibility that love can be packaged in a new, healthy way. And slowly, in time, she and I told Chris (and meant it), "*I love you.*"

Sometimes, it takes another person to patiently wait for you to stretch out, emerge from your fetal position, and be your true self — so they can show you that they have the capacity to be with all parts of you. Chris let me slowly emerge, helped me feel safe and seen, and chose to partner with me in ways I had not yet known were possible.

13

Step at a Time

All I need to do
is take
a single step —
and it usually
turns into two;
before I know it,
I've stepped into
a way of being
now
mighty
and true.
It no longer feels
scary —
it's just something
I do.
So I'll step
again,
as it turns
into two,

and I'll be
many more
steps toward
another thing
mighty
and new.

14

"You don't find Leadville; Leadville finds you."

The words of Ken Chlouber, founder of this "race across the sky," drifted through me as I ran toward Mayqueen aid station. As I moved forward on the rocky trail, the sun beginning to press against my face, I considered how this race had found me.

I can't say for certain where I first heard about the Leadville 100. As a high school and college runner, I had a faint idea that there was a subculture of runners who'd go for long, unbelievable-at-the-time miles. For someone who was training for the 5K on trails and the 800 meters on the track by running about thirty miles per week, I couldn't fathom a hundred miles in a week — let alone over the course of twenty-four hours. I'm sure I flipped my hand against the notion, claimed it was "crazy," and moved on.

The year 2020 changed my thoughts on it all, though. I was cooped up during lock down, watching more Netflix than anyone could ever need. I was antsy and looking for a dream to dream, so I spent hours trying to stay informed on the racial and societal injustices that were made glaringly apparent in that time. We lived several blocks from George Floyd Square and were doing what we could in our immediate neighborhood to feel both safe and actively involved. I fell into YouTube rabbit holes and went for long walks listening to podcasts, new music, and audio books.

And in that throb of seeking — and too much time on my hands — I discovered the ultra running universe over a glass of pinot noir.

Sally McRae. Harvey Lewis. Ann Trason. Courtney Dauwalter. Hellah. Rich Roll. Dylan Bowman. Kilian Jornet. Jim Walmsley. Camille Herron. Clare Gallagher. Devon Yanko. Andy Glaze. Tommy Rivers. I was unearthing name after name, extraordinary human after extraordinary human. And of them, so many women who were gritty and determined. I was smitten.

I made a conscious decision: I was going to become an ultra-runner. During those long, uncertain days of COVID, I started running again — but differently. Not to prove anything, not to punish or perfect, just to *feel*. Without races or pace goals, running slowly began to feel like a quiet return to myself. I wanted to see how far I could go, too.

Running has a way of opening doors for me. As a teen and young adult, I developed a sense of belonging and autonomy on my high school and college cross country and track teams. It was a place I could feel important, special — outside the walls of my home. In my twenties, I trained for marathons in places like New York City, Austin, and Chicago. Running was an essential part of me.

But it was also a protective armor.

My favorite kind of run in my twenties was the kind that kept me alone, on fire, and plugged into my headphones as I welcomed the grind. My Strava and other social media pages were a shallow refuge of connection. Little likes from fellow runners were temporary balms, my brain mistaking the dopamine surge for community, but my body was not safely communing. My body did not quite feel like mine.

The thing we love can become tangled and misshapen, misused and abused, because we actually need something greater — a deeper form of healing. I didn't need running to love me. It couldn't because I needed something more — something vast and deep and rich and visceral. I didn't have the words for it at the time, but I felt it. There was a rock in the deepest part of my belly after every run that I got good at ignoring.

But that rock was a message. My solar plexus, the ganglia of nerves in the pit of the stomach, was alerting the rest of my nervous system to "Please, pay attention."

That message became a part of how I felt on the daily, becoming my normal. And so, it became easy to ignore. It became easy to run: run hard, run fast, run without rest, run myself to the ground.

In the fifth grade, we were given an assignment to draw our biggest dream for our Big Person Self. I had just watched an older sister finish the Boston Marathon. I also trekked out a few times for run-walks with my dad, and I loved playing games like Red Light Green Light, Red Rover, and Capture the Flag. I loved being in motion. So, I drew myself at the finish line of the Boston Marathon, arms in the air, victorious.

A decade later, I qualified for Boston at the New York City Marathon, and then again in Chicago. I was as fast as ever, and fit. Every day, I slammed out workouts on the treadmill during the Minnesota winter. But, I was slamming workouts with a traumatized body and neglecting to balance that work with true, good rest.

By the time I toed the line for Boston, I was exhausted. The training burned me out and I was fatigued by the disconnect I felt from the body I had built over the months. Adult acne spread across my face. Insomnia bloomed. My arms and legs flared with the red splotches of tinea, a stress-induced skin fungus. When I was intimate with a partner, all I felt was a hollow sadness. Food barely interested me and I shut myself off from friendships, easily ignoring texts and calls. I ran a tough race, clocking a personal best time by a minute, but truthfully, I didn't enjoy almost every step of that marathon.

However, as I crossed the finish line, I managed to tap my heart for the little kid dreamer inside of me and whispered, *"We did it."* Even in the midst of deep exhaustion, I found an ounce of love toward myself.

When the ultra running community began knocking at my door during lock down, I was in a much different head space with my running. I was ready to shape shift from the once-intense approach I had into a more fluid, supportive one. I was hopeful for a remedy for my soul that somehow included running in a way that could work for me instead of against me.

If we go searching for a balm to our hurt, it's no surprise that it emerges from the woven fabric of several places: the research we do, the people and influences who appear, the curiosity that builds, the excitement of possibility that buzzes. When the mind is primed with curiosity, it's a lot easier to recognize an open door for what it is.

So, when I joined a virtual meeting in 2021 and heard the Life Time Foundation speak about the Leadville 100 and their athletes who raised money as they trained for it — I was ready. This was my way in. A nudge from the universe. A door to walk through. In my most recent history, I had survived a bad relationship and the whole of 2020; I'd broken patterns of choosing the wrong men; I had reclaimed my relationship with running as a more balanced one. Yes, I had overcome a lot — but I hadn't yet surpassed, healed, embodied the fullness of strength I knew I possessed. I was ready, and it was time. I returned home to myself just in time to recognize the opportunity of Leadville and follow the trail she laid out for me.

I immediately sent the speaker from the Foundation an email, and within a few days we had a call set up to get me started as a Foundation athlete.

The mission of the Foundation was simple: to get healthy food and movement opportunities to kids across America. It was one of a few organizations that offered a fundraising option to get into the race (the others include The Leadville Legacy Foundation and First Descents). Athletes hoping to get a bib entry otherwise went through a lottery system and waited to be selected. I was more than happy to fund raise to ensure my spot at the starting line.

A plan developed. I would volunteer at the 2022 Leadville 100 with the Life Time Foundation and set my sights on running the race the following year.

I could feel it right then and there: Leadville was different. It wasn't just an ultra — it was a high-altitude proving ground. A town with a mythos, a race with real grit. Something about it felt sacred, like it demanded something primal and powerful from every runner who showed up. I didn't just want to run far — I wanted to run *up and* into something that had the possible formula to change me.

I found Leadville. Or, more appropriately — Leadville found me.

I boarded a plane that August, landing in Denver at midnight in the pouring rain to witness what the Leadville 100 was all about.

15

Note from the Trail

My shoes carried me here:
a long, loping trail
snaking its way upward to
the heartbeat of a mountain.
My feet hear the cyclist
long before my eyes spot him.
Together we breathe heat
as his wheels scrape and slide by,
me leaping to the the trail's edge
steadying torso against an aspen.
Leaves dance with alpine wind,
the shake of schoolyard games.
I am flung through time
to my ten-year-old body:
Clink of ice in sweet lemonade
on a splintered wood deck
cloudless sky, sunburned back,
living to play outside.
In the church of forest

a steady hum of sound now:
swarms of bug music
gasps of whispered wind in bramble
kettle corn pops of insects.
I move with Earth's
heaving chest
in the rib cage of a mountain trail.
I know:
I'll get to where I'm going.

16

The Trees All Know My Name

One year before Race Day: Volunteering at the 2022 Leadville 100

The dirt road curved from one side of the historic Twin Lakes village to the other. At one end, the general store vibrated with customers who exited with coffee cups, water, and snacks in hand. The namesake glacial lakes sparkled, reflecting mountains, paddle boarders, and a smattering of clouds. At the other end, a trail dropped abruptly into the village, welcoming runners to a parted sea of erupting fanfare.

This was the Twin Lakes Aid Station, 37.9 miles into the Leadville 100. I was about to meet up with the Life Time Foundation team and take part in my first-ever Leadville 100 experience — from the sidelines.

My day began in Frisco, my trip's home base and a thirty-minute-or-so drive from Leadville. I'd opted not to wake up for the 4 a.m. start and instead took in some much-needed sleep before heading out. I arrived in the Twin Lakes area with immediate astonishment. It was my first time seeing the lakes set against the mountain range. A line of cars squeezed against the single road leading into town. I nudged my rental Jeep into the first available opening, pushed the engine button off, and sat still, taking it in. So, this was the Leadville 100.

So much history precluded my arrival. The first shotgun start to this race was back in 1983, five years before my arrival as child number seven of twelve. Forty-four runners took off that morning from Leadville (compared to about 600–700 starters today). This western town, with all its cowboy and mining charm, is known as the highest incorporated city in America, marking the Leadville 100 trail run as an oxygen-deprived venture that requires "guts, grit, and determination."

Leadville is an out-and-back course; therefore, what you experience on the way out, you get reversed on the way back to the finish. The hundred-mile trail leads runners through the forested Rocky Mountains, up and over Sugarloaf Pass, Mt. Elbert, and Hope Pass, ultimately turning them around at mile fifty in the ghost town of Winfield. Each participant climbs about 15,600 feet over the entirety of the race (and, of course, drops just as much, as they take on the same route home).

Much of the race is what's called "runnable." There are portions of paved roads, gorgeous drops down mountain passes, and jeep roads wide and open. It's imperative to begin the race with a steady-enough pace: runners who miss cutoff times at designated aid stations along the course are promptly escorted out of the competition. Outbound — heading toward Winfield — has a much tighter cutoff time expectation than

Inbound — heading home to the finish line. Mental strategy is needed just as much as physical preparation.

I caught wind that the most fantastic place to spectate was the Twin Lakes Aid Station. Sitting at the base of Hope Pass, runners receive sustenance from food and community before disappearing up the mountain. It would be another twenty miles before they would return to this haven. Many runners have a crew — a group of people dedicated to their well-being. Crews can meet their runner at major aid stations to feed them, take care of their feet, and offer a social uplift to an otherwise solo experience. Twin Lakes was one of two aid stations where crews posted up with tents, music, food, and fanfare (the other being Outward Bound at mile 23 and 77).

When I got out of the Jeep, I walked three-quarters of a mile up the road into town. On my way, people were loading coolers and piling utility wagons with supplies. Others were asleep in their front seats, caps pulled over their eyes. The closer I got to the village, the greater the throb of sound and play. People lined the dirt road to the left and right. Many had tents erected, complete with folded chairs, tables of food, and collections of cold drinks. Music rolled from a nearby business, Twin Lakes SUP & Cycle, and the employees passed around sloshing Solo cups, a bottle of tequila in hand. I wondered if any runners would partake in the bottle as they ran through town.

Encircling the village and lakes were the mountains of the Collegiate Peaks sub-range of the Sawatch Range. Lush, each was a mass of rippling leaves and pools of net-caught sunshine. They rose firm and tall, cradling with mastery the humanity roused at their base. The sky opened up in a brilliant blue, barely a cloud and many a bird swooping through it. The party began to melt from my perception as I felt rooted into the dirt road and my shoulders drooped, relaxed. The elixir of wood and dirt and wildflowers surrounding us.

A memory overtook me. Hazy, since memories are but half-truths and snapshots of a life behind us, colored only by the perspective we've got. The bees, the spankings, the whirlwind of growing up in a big family — and this:

It was the morning before my First Communion, a rite for young Catholics as they received the Eucharist (considered the "body of Christ") for the first time. Hours before the ceremony, my dad invited me hiking. Mom had put rollers in my hair, pulled tight with bobby pins. Wearing an oversize T-shirt, neon bicycle shorts, and scrunched socks stuffed into dirty sneakers, I followed Dad.

The day had a specialness to it. It'd be the first time I was able to receive the Eucharist at church, a blessing my parents took seriously. In my endeavor to be a good girl — to feel loved and accepted — the day felt important to me, too. I felt a deep reverence in my eight-year-old body that morning.

Dad drove to a trail head nearby and cut the engine. Jumping out of the truck, we walked into the woods, Dad pointing out all kinds of vegetation and wildlife along the way. This was my favorite version of him: walking on dirt, watching nature unfold, becoming part of a cool, bright morning. I liked that he knew what type of bugs were under the rocks and how high the fish in the stream could jump. Pressing my hand and ear onto rough tree bark, I listened for a heartbeat I was so sure was there. Sunshine spotlights broke through the tree line, announcing everything my father pointed to. That mushroom — serious. Those birds — special. This walk with my dad — holy.

The upcoming religious ceremony was good, right and important, he told me. He placed his hand on my back and, with a proud chest, began to pray a Hail Mary aloud. If he said so, I believed it.

"When you grow up, you can be a mommy or a nun," my mother told me that morning, my father nodding along in agreement.

Back home, a lace white dress and veil hung in a closet, waiting for their First Communion moment. Like a bride, I'd walk down the church aisle, wearing the color of purity and carrying flowers. Like a nun, I'd tuck my chin, solemn and obedient to my chest, allowing the veil to cover the curls on my head.

For now, in that moment, I got to be a little kid learning how to identify her God in the trees. And those trees all knew my name.

Two decades later, I stared into the mountains at the edge of Twin Lakes. Splashes of light. Special. Serious. The familiar feelings from that walk in the woods swept through me and, to no one but myself, I mentally pointed.

That's Mt. Elbert. And that's Hope Pass, I noted as my gaze followed the light.

Leaving Minneapolis and boarding a plane for this long week-
end, I had an urge for reverence. *What is holy to me?* I thought in
the weeks prior while sorting through laundry, washing dishes,
and staring out the same smudged kitchen window.

At Twin Lakes Aid Station, it was a party. Margaritas instead
of blessed wine and laughing side hugs instead of the Sign of
Peace found at Catholic services. Shades and caps replaced
purity veils, and the dirt road down the middle of the village
opened wide, a ready aisle for the procession of runners.

Aid stations — especially an aid station like this one — are
reminders of how we belong, how we are loved, and how
essential ritual is in the midst of hardship. It's church. Families
and friends gathered, waiting for their runner. When they
arrived, broken and dispirited, their people flew into action.
They enveloped their runners in bear hugs, showered them
with encouragement, refueled with food, massaged worn-out
feet, and popped painful blisters — and finally sent them on
their way up toward Hope Pass.

This is my kind of holy, I thought, as I began to look for the Life
Time Foundation crew with whom I was to spend the day.

I began to walk through the crowd. Across the dirt, an icon
laughed with her group of friends. It was Courtney Dauwalter,
one of the best ultra runners of our time. She oozed comfort,
sliding past the tents, a permanent grin thriving on her face.
Instead of robes on a powerful man of the church, here was

a woman in long basketball shorts, socks pulled up well past her ankles, and dirt smears on her calves. Her running resume: impressive. Both a leader and an icon.

I observed others notice her too on their own walkabouts. Some folks extended a handshake or a hello; others turned to their companions and gushed. I made eye contact with her, offered a head nod, and slipped our encounter into my pocket for safekeeping.

I wondered what it must be like to be so known, so seen, so respected. At a race like this, Courtney seemed superhuman. Divine.

Ah, how easy, I caught my mind as it twirled into thought. How easy it is to misidentify other humans as untouchable. In my experience, Catholicism does this well. Priests (men) seem to be granted immunity, held as sacred representations of God. I had a lifetime of sharing my misdeeds (sins) to priests to ask for forgiveness; as well as Sunday after Sunday staring up at the pulpit, listening to them tell me how to live a pure life. I had learned (falsely) that they were the authority on my life, standing between me and my experience of God. I had learned (falsely) that I could not commune with what was holy without male guidance.

And, in succumbing to that power dynamic, I somehow learned (again, falsely) that I was less than. I forgot how to tune into the sacred experience always unfolding around me. Then, this place, tucked atop Colorado, was waking me to a new reality.

I watched as someone easily approached Courtney. They spoke with their entire body, an easy comfort. My eyes flitted past the pair and scanned the crowded sidelines. This was happening everywhere: hugs, handshakes, conversation. All kinds of bodies, and all ranges of ages. No one preaching or shaming, no pulpits or hierarchy, as far as I could tell.

Possibility swelled in me: *I am an ultra runner.*

An energized throb of celebration rippled through the crowd as the lead athlete ran through, as though sparked, molecule by molecule, creating something enormous. Something bigger than all of us.

This wasn't just a party or a simple aid station in a hundred-mile race.

This is a holy space, it occurred to me.

Then, I felt it more than I thought it:

I belong here.

17

Mountain Town

I've never been, yet
it's a homecoming.
The fog-tipped peaks,
signaling weather over trails
that tuck left and right,
up and through,
and out the tree line again.
Some places
you just belong.
Some places
have spoken to you before—
in photographs, in stories.
Some places
have room for you.
Here I am,
in a mountain town,
and the trees
all know my name.

18

Ben Rolls with Jesus

January before Race Day

Pineapple smoothie escaped from its straw and dribbled onto my chin. If you were to drive past me you'd see my feet planted on the dashboard and a grin the size of a large pizza on my face. It was January in Hawaii, the year before Colorado. Chris was driving and I was a happy passenger princess.

The phone rang in my palm over the swoosh of tropical breeze. I didn't look at the screen right away. I was on vacation. I was actively forgetting my concerns, chasing the sunset toward the beach. It was all new — a freshly born moment, wet with possibility and untouched by the world as I knew it.

Newness thrills me. Beginnings reel me in like a caught fish — dangling, excitable. The starting over, once again, excites me: the first step onto the Spanish Steps, the initial crunch of summer dirt on a loping trail, pulling up to the house that's not yet a home. That first-day-of-school feeling with naked notebooks and an opaque ruler stuffed into a pencil case, the price tag sticker still stuck, untouched by dirty playground fingers.

I like to wonder who I will end up becoming by choosing to arrive somewhere new. It's electric. I get a rush just thinking about the freshness of change and the adventures it can take me on. I've dumped boyfriends and gotten back together with them just so I could feel the beginning all over again. The thrill of a trail not trekked and the maps app on my phone directing me to a mystery address.

What I've since discovered is that I can learn to like middles. The process. The bumps and the bruises from when we get knocked down, or how the new car smell loses its freshness along the way. Getting lost and having to ask for directions — because inevitably, this is where we meet others. Others on a path, a reckoning, an adventure of their own. I become part of their story and they, mine. I learned that I like the kind of people I meet in the middle. I like the plainness of it all — the browns and oranges and the rusty reds and that color that reminds you of waiting in line at the grocery store as a child. Middles are the only thing that get us from the start to the end.

Even though I had experienced endings throughout my life time, they still remain especially difficult.

My phone was still ringing. I scrunched my nose at the screen, the name of a running acquaintance popping up.

"He never calls me," I said and turned the music down in the car, setting my smoothie into the car holder. I answered.

"Hello?"

Time slowed.

And then, it began to spiral — catapulting forward — and I had no choice but to tumble along with it.

After a few brief words I hung up and pressed my forehead into my hands, hard, as if I could press my way out of that moment and into the jungle heat of the island.

"Ben's dead," I said, more so that I could grasp the words than to let Chris know. Ben, my running friend, was suddenly gone.

* * *

Ben fell into stride with me during the Birkie Trail Marathon just a year and a half prior to the phone call in late September. I was caught up in my head, as usual, and oblivious to the other runners. A sunrise start time meant the trees were still yawning, the birds singing them awake. My body was warming up and my breath formed clouded puffs. A bush rustled as I passed and a critter I'll never meet properly shot out, fleeing the chaos of stampeding humans, startling me. I quickened. Within seconds, I was behind another runner and forced to slow down because there was no room to pass on the tight path. It was early yet and I could relax in the first few miles — although, I didn't want to. I clawed at my pack to find a slice of gum to distract me.

The runner turned his head as he heard me approach, saying, "And what about you!" It was more an exclamation than a question.

I like to listen to others talk during a run, not be the one talking. When I was in grade school, my favorite activity was to find a hiding place so I could eavesdrop on phone calls. I overheard breakups, complaints, and juicy gossip; it's how I first learned about the world.

"What about me?" I asked.

"What's your running story?" His elbows pressed back with each step forward as though they were poking me for a friendly answer.

When I'm feeling introverted on the trail, I sometimes stick to the easy answers. Only offering one or two words to match my mood. But for some reason that day, I decided to give a little more than usual.

"I'm one of twelve kids and well, we all ran. Hand-me-down running shoes are cheaper than hockey equipment," I offered. "And I grew to really love the sport. After high school and college, I kept running. Mostly marathons now. Just getting into trails."

He all but clapped with glee. "A lifetime runner!" he exclaimed. "COVID got me into it. I started running during lock down."

"I'm Ben," he said as he sidestepped a protruding root with a playful hop, impressively nimble for his forty-something year old body. "Watch out for that!"

I laughed. "I'm Barbara."

Question after question, we traded off leading on the single-track trail. He asked me about running, life, my faith, and my upbringing. Every so often his watch would beep and he'd slow his pace, "Heart rate!" he explained with a lopsided grin.

It wasn't long before we got into faith. "I roll with Jesus," he said, playfully shrugging. Religion got him through the hard times, he shared. It gave him a sense of purpose, a community to connect with, and a way to give praise for all he was grateful for. As he spoke, I imagined my parents. Two young people trying to make it in the world, seeking security and unconditional love. Catholicism, the Church, the rituals and prayers: a lifeline for them, a confinement for me. In many ways, it helped them raise twelve incredible kids.

Although it wasn't the path I would take as an adult — I couldn't claim to "roll with Jesus" — I understood. And Ben helped me get there.

* * *

Back in Hawaii, I looked down at my hands. The veins were pulsing blue, and my nails at the tip of each finger were short, stumped. I laced one hand into the other. I have my mother's hands, I remember thinking. My chest swelled, a familiar ache washing through it. I pressed down on one of the protruding veins and traced it back and forth. No longer was I in a rental car on Oahu digesting news of a friend's passing. I was in the living room of the old farmhouse, curled up on my mother's lap as she read a story to a pile of children who were crowding her. A wood stove crackled and heaps of freshly chopped wood awaited their fate. I was tracing her veins as she read, pressing the life force of her blue blood back and forth, back and forth.

Chris and I spent the afternoon bent over drinks at Kalapawai Market. Just yesterday, one table over, we sat, sweaty from climbing Koko Crater — a no-longer-used railway trail up a dormant volcano. We had marveled at the task, elated with the life dripping from our bodies. Famished, we had ordered fish tacos; drinks eased our thirst. Clinking together frothy beer and sparkling sangria, we felt invincible, alive.

This time, we were somber. Although Chris had only met Ben once or twice, he knew how meaningful the friendship was to me. The buzz of the cafe was the same, and the drinks were the exact order from the day prior. But now, they tasted like what-the-fuck and holy-hell. My sweet sangria tasted of shock.

* * *

Right around mile thirteen of the Birkie Marathon, Ben had nudged me.

"You haven't run an ultra yet?" he exclaimed after I confessed that this marathon was my farthest endeavor to date. "You gotta run an ultra. Do Wild Duluth.; it's a 50K. It's in two weeks. You're fit — you can totally do it."

As we trotted onward, I mentally massaged the suggestion. His enthusiasm made the notion fathomable. The further we went down the trail, the more Ben's light pressed its way inside of me — and in that moment, I was ready to receive it.

"I guess I'll see you there!" My heart rate quickened at the idea and inevitably all kinds of intrusive thoughts began to try and worm their way into my mind to spoil it all. *Be here now,* I coached myself.

We continued on, one foot in front of the other, sharing time.

I took a wrong turn mid-race after surging ahead of Ben and ended up clocking around 29 miles — 3 bonus miles. It was as if the universe was trying to prove to me that I was capable. I burst into tears at the finish as Chris collected me into a giant hug.

I signed up for the Wild Duluth 50K that evening.

Two weeks later, I showed up to the Superior Hiking Trail and took on the gnarly, winding, hilly trails from Jay Cooke Park up to Duluth, Minnesota. Those fifty kilometers were grueling. I wasn't accustomed to the amount of power hiking I had to do. Hill after hill taunted me and all I could do was drive my way up, hands on my thighs, bent over my lungs. When the terrain shifted down or leveled out, I could pick up my legs and run.

Someone handed me a watermelon with salt at an aid station, and later on I led a group of runners down the wrong trail as I got distracted watching my footing. In the last mile, I fell into stride with a college kid and managed to haul it into the finish.

Ben was at the finish line. He had started the race with me, but a nagging injury forced him to call it early and step out of the race. He held a beer in his hand, nudging it toward me as I sank my hands into my knees. A bee landed on the can's lip, and I swiped it away with a weary hand. Mindless, unafraid.

It was that finish line that hooked me. The process — all those middle moments, all the relentless forward progress during the race — got me to a land of smiling, happy people with cold beers in hand and friendly dogs on leashes ready to lick the salt off me. Hours of movement and mental chatter, turning my legs over, sidestepping roots and rocks, and negotiating with my mind in an effort to stay in the race — it all got me to the shore of Lake Superior underneath the inflatable finishers arch.

I couldn't walk right for the following two days, but I welcomed the hobble. I wore the maroon race hoodie for three days straight. And for a solid week, I leaned my race bib against a pile of books on my home office desk at eye level. I wanted to bask in it, keep the feeling alive and well, as I worked.

Ben and I met up to run at Lebanon Hills in Eagan, Minnesota many times after that race. We chatted about life, loss, religion, and racing. He listened to my stories, and told me some of his. He was especially excited to hear I was toying with the idea of running a hundred miler.

"Can't wait to run Leadville with ya!" Ben crowed one morning during the summer of 2022 as we ran through the pouring rain. We snapped a selfie to celebrate the moment.

That was one of our last runs together.

* * *

I cannot, I slumped with my sangria in Hawaii, *I cannot sit around. I cannot remain the same. I cannot have a year that isn't worth remembering. I cannot, I cannot, I cannot.*

I looked up from my glass and caught Chris inspecting me carefully.

"Let's make the most of this trip," I mumbled.

I scraped the chair back and stood up, pulling the bottom of my shorts down from their scrunched position at my upper thighs. Chris took my hand, his eyes concerned, and we walked out into the final few days of our vacation.

19

My Friend Died Today

A week ago
really
but he died
again today.
I went to text him
an invite:
"Let's go run"
and again
he died,
softly in my hands –
delete
delete
delete –
on just
another Saturday.

20

The Moment It Clicked

February before Race Day

After returning to Minnesota from my volunteering trip to Colorado — and then learning of Ben's sudden passing while in Hawaii — I didn't exactly know my next step. Days, then weeks, slipped by. The weather dipped down to a miserable double-digit below zero. I went to Ben's Celebration of Life with another running friend, Paxton. The clock ticked toward midnight in late February, and I lay in a tired heap on the bed. The blankets seemed too thin, the pillow too flat, and I felt like my world was inching by too slow.

Everything stacked, then cracked, in my mind.

During the pandemic, I was propelled into a crisis support role at my place of employment. As a holistic performance coach with a master's in integrative health and well-being Coaching, I was on a small team that supported mental and emotional well-being. I went from coaching folks toward their professional and personal goals to applying emotional tourniquets for both furloughed and remaining team members. In a world of so many unknowns and potential threats, I gave the tools I knew to my colleagues: cognitive thought shifting, meditation, breathing, and everyday reminders for self-care. I created a safe place for my clients to emote. Every day was a trial of doing my best — but my best hovered around a slim ten percent of my norm.

Many months of survival status brought us to relationship fatigue for Chris and I. Chris experienced panic attacks, on alert in our Minneapolis neighborhood during protests and strife. Between my clients and keeping it together at home, I felt more like a caregiver than a partner. I was ready to run — to end it, so we could both move forward and begin again. That questioning of staying together had become a regular part of our relationship. I had one foot in — and one foot out.

I scheduled a virtual hypnosis session. Although this was my first experience with this form of therapy (outside of using a self-administered app), I was feeling more open than skeptical. I understood enough regarding neuroplasticity and regulating the nervous system to surrender to this healing modality.

The healer helped me become acquainted with the lived experiences in my body. She helped me see what I was holding onto as memory and, with her guidance, I reshaped those moments. A two-hour session rushed by like water spilling through cupped hands.

Chilled and hypnotized in the Twin Cities' suburbs, the greatest sensation I had was an ache to feel loved. Like a newborn, I wanted to curl my fingers around it and hold onto the felt sense that I was important — that I mattered.

This wasn't a new feeling. All my life I have felt as though others were more deserving of love, were of greater importance, were more worthy than me. It's certainly impacted my work, my creativity, and my relationships.

As the middle child, I shared everything — a bunk bed and a bedroom, my parents' affection, and every piece of clothing. My sense of individuality was clouded by the reality that many of my siblings had similar interests to me, which often seemed even grander, better, more important. Even my birthday was only mine until kindergarten, when my twin sisters were born on that day. My graduation ceremonies also belonged to my Irish twin, Joe. In a world where I got good at sharing, I also became skilled at falsely believing I was less than.

Throughout my twenties, I often found myself feeling emptied and low, in search of something greater than myself to help lift me up to a sense of wholeness. Simply running through a finish line or getting into a relationship wasn't enough to soothe this hurt. I needed love. I needed healing. I needed my own ongoing experience of holy.

The hypnosis session brought much of this to the surface. The hypnotist murmured instructions through the screen. Relaxed, I fully gave in.

I saw it: the challenges that little me had lived through and the imprints they left on my body. I felt how easy it was for me to feel sorry for myself, to sit back and wait for someone to love me how I wanted to be loved. And I saw how much I passed blame and shame onto my partner expecting him to know how to love a body that could not feel truly safe within herself.

An early memory burst forward: My father throwing a plate of food across the dining room because my sister didn't want to eat her squash. Explosive, sudden — scary to a little kid. Dried yellow squash, sticking to the stained glass of the ceiling's Tiffany lamp, remained there for the rest of that year. Later I would learn this was a combination of piled on work stress and the exhausted need for us kids to behave.

The hypnotherapist guided me to feel into it, and then create a feeling and image that my inner child needed. A yellow glow emerged, softening the sounds of shatter and yelling, absorbing the squash and the broken plate and my father's face. A step forward toward healing.

Even midst these angry moments, all I wanted was to spend time with my dad. At every opportunity, I woke before the sun to go fishing or hiking with him. And then later in the week, without warning, his fury changed him again. It was confusing to a kid. How could the man I loved so much — who woke me up at dawn to go on a day's adventure, who prayed dutifully at church every week — how could that man transform so fast?

I coped, as children do and I remembered turning to the magical realms of imagination, book-reading, and playing for hours outside. My siblings and I would spend many waking moment in the back field and woods behind the farmhouse, forging trails and building forts, creating whole worlds. Summertime was spent catching tadpoles and running barefoot; winters with ice skating on woodland ponds and trekking to the big sled hill a mile and a half away. When not outside, we pressed our noses into books, doing our best to behave.

There was a healing magic to the nature around our home. I am grateful to the buzz of bugs, the thick bark on trees meant for climbing, and the wet, slippery moss on the creek bed that held me when things got unsettled. When I was in the woods, I felt spaciousness, free of insignificance, free of being a good girl, free from expectations to behave.

I was just able to be.

As a child, I attempted to create my version of safety in the quiet of solitude. I'd sometimes curl up in the coat closet and listen to my dad walk from room to room. At night, I'd pull the covers over my head and get lost in books with a dimming flashlight. Midday, I'd go up to the tree house and wait there, sometimes for hours, to see if anyone would come looking for me.

All of that turning inward as a youngster left imprints on my body, heart, and mind. Imprints that simply became part of who I was over time. Imprints that I could lovingly, gradually take a good and careful look at many years later in my life. Imprints that I could love and heal, every day, any time.

I felt urgency ever since I hung up the phone in Hawaii. Not only did that phone call alert me to the frailty of life, but also the crippling obedience we surrender to the thoughts of disbelief in ourselves: *I could never* and *I'm not the type of person who...*

One of the last conversations Ben and I had was about the Leadville 100 trail run. I hadn't made concrete plans about it, other than possibly signing up for the race. Ben lit up like a little boy when I shared my desire to run it.

"You're going to crush it," he gushed. "Tell me what you decide to do, and I'll come hang — whether to train with you or pace you on the day." Unwavering, I-believe-in-you support. How I wish this for everyone.

"Breathe it all out," the hypnotist guided in a voice between a whisper and a murmur, our session coming to a close.

As I exhaled, I was warmed by a thought: *Who are you uninter-rupted?* I was once asked this by a mentor. She didn't mean just by time, or commitments, or others. Who would you be if you weren't interrupted by negative thoughts or limiting beliefs or the stories you tell yourself? I think we are meant to entertain that beautiful thought in order to expand our sense of self. In order to grow.

Poetry gushed from within me that evening from a now un-blocked channel. A timeline was born. I was momentarily uninterrupted — the freshness of emotional reset rich and vital. Winter wind wailed outside the front stoop and my dog curled up dutifully at my feet. Something rattled loose inside me, and a tiny seed, planted long ago, was beginning to spread roots and grow.

Uninterrupted.

Then, called to action.

Talking with Chris, we established an opportunity for space. Every fiber in my being wanted to move out to Colorado as soon as possible and train at altitude. I wanted not just to be physically ready for Leadville — but to also retreat from the strain in Minneapolis. And more than a want, I needed a way to get to know myself — and my kind of holy — better.

I had to do it on my own. I had to run.

Chris, supportive as ever, encouraged me. Even though it meant we would be apart for five months, he was willing to let me go, hopeful that our relationship could benefit in the long-term. Looking back, I clearly see that this was a beautiful expression of love for me.

I created a Facebook post asking if I knew anyone in Summit County, Colorado where I could move that summer to train. Friends rallied and information exchanged. Days later, I was on the phone with a homeowner in Alma, a statutory town in the High Country with a population of barely 300. She had a room and an office space to rent at a reasonable price at 11,000 feet altitude by Hoosier Pass. It came with three roommates, a parking space, and thin air to sleep in.

And I could move in on April 1st.

21

Relationship Status

If you took a sip of me today
you'd realize how flat I've become.
"Where's the fizz?" you'd protest,
"Where's the bubble, the spray, the play?"
You can't send me back to whence I came.
The kitchen is closed;
the busboys went home;
the fan above the stove cut quiet.
We now stand in the light
from the cracked refrigerator door,
a curtain of white breaking in
as we rummage
for something new to be.
All the world is quiet,
the mice in the back yard
have raised their whiskers,
a possum passes like a ghost.
I reach for the place
where your heart went wild,

foraging in the moonlight for clues
of whom we've become since
the shake of a pandemic,
the swirl of lock down
a Revolution,
sweat of uncertainty
wet in our hands.
Remember?
You stayed up all night
with whiskey courage.
I lay breathless in bed.
Our town was on fire.
We did the best that we could.
We realize now
the fizz
the pop
are now gone.
We grasp for something more.

22

Moving In and Holding On

April before Race Day

The icy road kept winding.

Clutching the steering wheel of my 2001 Subaru Forester, I tensed as it rattled up the mountain. To my right, the road dropped off, a cavern of sloping mountainside, nary a barrier to keep me on the road. Gulping, I kept my eyes straight ahead. Every cell in my body wanted to drink up the magical ascension of land all around me but I sure as shit had to focus.

It was April Fool's Day, my mother's birthday, and snow blanketed the sea of pine and aspen. The night before, I was nervously tucked into bed at an AirBnB in Omaha Nebraska, wondering what this moment would look like, feel like, be like.

I barely slept in that rented basement room – instead, I rose from the bed at midnight and undressed in front of the standing mirror. I looked at every inch of my body, turning round to inspect skin and fat, hair and nails, muscle and scars. A body. My body. Vulnerable in the Midwest moonlight.

A small pile of my sweatpants and T-shirt lay on the floor, underwear kicked to the side of the room. I drew my hands to my face and touched the darkened lines beneath my eyes. My fingers traced my cheeks, following the weary pathways of tears fallen then up to the crowfeet crinkles at my temples formed from how I smile with my whole face. I turned, chin over shoulder, inspecting the curve of my spine leading to a strong backside. The rolling hills of my skin, exposed.

No turning back now, I thought, a bit dramatic.

I let out a whimper.

What do I even want? Naked in Nebraska, I stared at the mirror: rounded thighs, dimpled butt, one knee larger than the other from a past injury. Doubt prickled me, goosebumps rising on my exposed skin.

I picked up my phone and texted my friend Hallie.

"I'm 8 hours away from the CO place. Can't believe I'm doing this."

Within a minute, my phone buzzed: "I believe it." I was surprised she was awake.

Air whooshed out of my lungs and I dropped into a heap on the floor.

OK, the mind prompted, *OK. I'm willing. I am willing to try.* Notes to self I had written over and over again throughout the years began to take over my mental script. *I can believe in myself. I am willing to mess up, to learn, to grow. I am willing to be independent, to do this on my own. No one else is going to do this for me.*

I slept in fits, waking every hour on the hour. Each time, I peered out the bedside window to check on the Subaru. She was stuffed, my belongings pressed against the windows, parked on the street. Exposed, bursting with "too much," a bit like how I felt. Unable to release my anxiety, my mind spun thoughts of someone stealing my car. Sweat dampened my hairline, and my shirt stuck to my skin. Fortunately, no one swiped the car; unfortunately, I did not get a great rest that night.

Before my alarm could go off, I was up making coffee, throwing toiletries back into my backpack, and then scooting into the front seat. By that afternoon, I was driving up the mountain toward Hoosier's Pass with a small line of better-equipped-for-this-part-of-town vehicles towed behind me, impatient.

My phone pinged to say turn was approaching. The Continental Divide sign greeted me at the top of the Pass with its soon-recognizable ultra runner posting. I was halfway between the Atlantic and Pacific. *Halfway.* I sputtered out a half laugh. How appropriate; I was halfway between everything, it seemed. Between dark and light, healing and pain, grudge and forgiveness, then and now.

I crested the top and followed the road down the other side. The impatient queue of cars soared past at the first sign of the white dotted line. This would happen all summer long. I got used to being overtaken because of the lack of horsepower in my car's 2001 engine. My chest surged and a sob half formed. I was two minutes away from the tip of Lakeview Drive, my new home.

I swallowed, taking a few steady but insufficient breaths. I could really feel the altitude. After turning onto the county road, I checked my high-tech watch to get an idea of how high up I really was: 11,000 feet. My head spun and the windshield glossed with my mental fog. I had been living right around 900 feet (barely) in Minnesota for the last almost-decade. This was the most extreme jump my body had experienced. I turned into the country road and it immediately began to climb even higher.

"Shit!" My car sputtered and stopped moving forward. Imprisoning the tires were piled of ankle-deep slush and snow. I was stuck. It was a quarter mile up to the cabin where I was about to sign a six-month lease. But instead of holding a pen, I was spinning my wheels in the early April snowfall. My worn-down tires were diligently proving how worthless they were in this weather.

A lone truck pulled up behind me and waited for me to move.

"Uh, I'm not going anywhere," I mumbled, rolling down my window. I was tired and starting to feel bad for myself. It was a long drive and I was almost there. But, I wasn't sure what I needed to do to get moving again. I hate feeling incapable and, in that moment, I felt all of its burden.

I waved the truck on, and it began to edge past me, my embarrassment halting any possible effort of asking for help. Fortunately, it slowed and a man leaned out the front.

"Ya got chains for those tires?" he asked.

Red-faced, I replied, "No. I'm trying to get up this hill. Nothing seems to work."

"Here, let me see what I got." He disappeared into his backseats and then emerged with a small yellow shovel. "Let's clear ya a bit so you can backtrack," he said.

Seconds later, he was behind my car shoveling the slush away from my spun-out tires. With a nod, he clambered back into his truck and took off. It was just enough shoveling that I could reverse and move back down the road to where I first turned. Looking at the steering wheel, I realized that my hands were turning white with pressure. I loosened my grip, closed my eyes, and willed away my tears.

Then, Colleen arrived.

Colleen was the rental manager and fortunately knew the approximate timing of my arrival. She pulled up in her SUV next to me, rolled down the window, and shouted: "Back up, press the gas and follow me! Don't lose your momentum!" With that, she floored it and ripped up the impossibly slick road.

No time to think, only time to trust.

I did what she said and flew up behind her. I yanked the steering wheel in a frenzy as my car desperately maneuvered the slushy uphill. I was flooded with a remarkable sense of power, thrill, and the wild abandon of acting alongside fear. It was like getting on the swings at the amusement park for the first time at seven years old. I had kicked and screamed as the chairs lifted up off the ground, tearful at the uncertainty of height and speed colliding. But once we started spinning in the air, I was elated, awestruck. I love a good ride.

I have no idea how I didn't just go flying off the deep steep edges of the road that day. Thankfully, I somehow stayed the course, followed the lead of capable Colleen, and within a few minutes I was parked right out front of the cutest mountain cabin there ever was. My heart felt like it was about to pound right out of my chest.

I started laughing.

Laughter is an excellent companion to fear, arriving alongside grief and anger, annoyance and difficulty. Laughter is our way of normalizing the moment, of lessening the burden and allowing ourselves to be so deliciously human and raw. I threw open my car door and, with big gulping breaths, reached out my hand to greet this new friend.

That is how I arrived, by the skin of my teeth, at an eighties-built cabin on the edge of Hoosier's Pass in Alma, Colorado, 11,000 feet altitude. My summer home. My training ground for the Leadville 100. My place of refuge to deepen my relationship with my mind and my body.

I can't believe I'm here. Again, a small voice inside me whispered as I stepped over the threshold, knocking the snow off my boots. I kicked them off and began to look around.

Another voice said, a bit more loudly, *I believe it.*

Thanks, Ben. I smiled to myself.

I took the pen from Colleen's outreached hand and signed my name on the dotted lease line. I was home for now.

After clearing out my Subaru and hoisting my belongings down the flight of stairs into my basement bedroom, I poured wine into the first available glass I could find. I knew that I would have three roommates, yet none of them home. With shallow breath, I tentatively nosed my way through the house.

Across from the stairway and past the kitchen, beneath the tall ceilings, a sliding door led out to a wood paneled deck. I pushed my way through it and gasped. Mt. Lincoln stood victorious, unmoving, tree house beyond an expanse of tall fir trees and aspens. Below the deck, chipmunks skittered, moose and bear tracks evident. Wind rippled their branches and ceremony of birdsong filled the thin air.

A whoosh of familiarity rushed through my veins.

When I close my eyes and dream up a peaceful setting where my body is at ease, my mind can slow down, and the worries of the world can wash away, I think about a tree house in my childhood backyard.

My dad was a resourceful man. His father was a carpenter and passed down the value of hard work and a good set of tools to his son. On the farmland of western Massachusetts, we had a life that was surrounded by the fruit of my dad's labor. After a full work week at the local correctional center where he created programming for inmates, he'd put his hands to work. He was flawed and, I'm sure due to the nature of his work, was dysregulated often; but the man taught me how to live well. He taught me how to work, how to create, and how to change the tide of a single day from simple stillness to excitement. One example of this was the tree house.

Behind our peeling white farmhouse, Dad piled up a large plot of sand every summer; we affectionately called this The Sand Pile. Retrieving sand by the truck-full from a nearby granite operation, he'd recruit us kids to help him shovel it off the red Ford's bed and onto the existing lot. The Sand Pile wrapped around an old oak tree and became the base for all our imaginative games. We built forts with moats, became chocolatiers for the afternoon, or acted out stories about dragons in faraway lands. We pulled cicada shells from the trees and used them as armor for the army men standing at attention and mixed water in buckets to create mud pie delights.

The Sand Pile was summertime.

One year, my dad built a tree house on The Sand Pile's tree. It had a basic panel floor and slatted sides with no roof to call its own; instead, the branches of the tree sheltered our little heads with elegance. To ensure we could climb up, my dad gave the tree house the ultimate ladder: an enormous fishing net made of weathered rope dug up from the Rhode Island beach side. He nailed it down at the fort's entrance and pulled it out slightly to create a concave ascension. Dad anchored it below with what I thought were railroad spikes, ensuring the net's steadiness.

It quickly became our summer home. Scurrying up and down that net, we could be anything: pirates one day, spiders another. Hours of imagination colored those long summer hours.

Across the way from the Sand Pile, an old green tractor sat at a standstill, inoperative – a time machine. Twisting the steering wheel and pushing the clutch and levers, we propelled ourselves back in time to the early pioneering days. We drummed up icy snow conditions on those summer days and then raced to our beloved tree house for protection from the elements. Reenacting everything we learned – from World War II to Lewis & Clark to Amelia Earhart – our tree house held us as we discovered and played.

Most important to me, though, this tree house became my refuge. Moments when I felt unseen and unloved, moments when I was scared or unsure, the tree house and her fishing net had arms big enough to hold me. Days in which I knew I could get into trouble and risk getting spanked, I would flee up the tree and sit with my back against the strong trunk top. I'd pull my knees into my chest and look out across the field that stood on our property. The robins and geese flew over me, then got smaller and smaller as they retreated beyond the trees at the field's edge.

I could be a bird, I remember thinking. I drew one alongside a small poem I had written. Even then, I had notebooks with me.

Little did I know, I was learning what it took for me to regulate my emotions. I was a little girl filled with anger and sorrow, confusion and grief. Some of this was unprocessed from grandparents passing and when I learned my mom miscarried a sibling who would have been older than me. Much of it was making sense of my emotions in a home where they felt too big.

I also felt unspoken confusion at messages of conditional love from my parents, teachers, and church leaders – for me to be a respectable "good girl" of whom Jesus, Mary, Joseph, the Holy Trinity, and all the perfect saints would be proud. That in order to be loved I had to stay still, be quiet, cross my legs, and be ladylike. I'd bargain with God some days, up in the tree, asking him to let me fly away with the geese. I promised I'd be a good girl; I'd offer to be ladylike and quiet and problem-free, all in exchange for the wings.

Those wooden boards held me. The sky went on forever, reminding me there was an expanse beyond my understanding of life: there was more, beyond the farmhouse. There were places to go and people to love. I'd fill composition notebooks with lists of what I wanted to do. I could be the one to go off into the world and create it all; it created a sense of ease in my worried, little body.

So, when I arrived at the cabin on the side of Hoosier's Pass, and stepped onto the plain boards and simple slatted sides of the back deck that overlooked the expanse of forever and a mountainside, I felt like a bird. I felt at ease. I opened my arms like wings.

The ten-year-old inside of me exhaled, the reality settling into her grown bones. She did it. She was a bird. She was living out the list in her notebook, all on her own.

I dropped onto the deck floor, wrapping my wings around my knees and pulling them into my chest. Backed up against the side of the home, I leaned my head against the tiles and broke into a soft, warm smile. No bargaining with God needed. No need to be a "good girl."

I was always good enough to be free, to be loved, to be me. It was time to unlearn anything to the contrary.

23

The Deep Knowing Within

April and May before Race Day

"Honestly, I just got a feeling it'll all work out," I pressed my chest out as I said it, my head throbbing with a slight altitude headache.

I was in a therapy session at the Alma cabin, the WiFi unreliable and breaking the tone between the pro and me. My therapist and I were dancing between past and present, naming and noticing what sensations I felt in my body. Making sense of my past. Speaking with kindness to my inner child. Preparing me for a future as I laid out my own red carpet and permitted myself to catwalk toward my north star.

The winter was holding on relentlessly to the side of the mountain that April into May. Every morning seemed to arrive with fresh snowfall. If the sun happened to show up, it created a landslide of slush and mud to navigate my Subaru through.

Altitude sickness held on to me with its own white-knuckle grip. Several days into my move, the headaches persisted. My nights consisted of waking up hourly to chug the Liquid IV at my bedside, sometimes refilling it once or twice before sunrise. As a devoted coffee drinker, I shifted to green tea since my beloved drink exacerbated the dehydration issue. I was, in a word, miserable.

But I knew it would pass. It was an alpine hangover that I needed to tend to, be patient with, and, with plenty of electrolytes, ride out with time.

My call ended and I flipped open my journal, tea steaming in hand. Well before arriving in Colorado, I'd created a habit of doing what's called Morning Pages. These are three pages of free writing done first thing in the morning to clear the mind, exercise the writing muscles, and access bits of creativity. I got the exercise from Julia Cameron's book, The Artist's Way (highly recommend for all my writers and artists!) and over the years it's become a staple as I begin my day each morning.

I haven't a clue really HOW it will work out. But I can trust myself. I just know I can, I wrote.

My journal held me: it knew my stories, my rationales, my epiphanies. Those pages allow me to explore in a messy way. I can be honest and real, allow the unfolding to take place at whatever pace it needed to. I could write a thought and challenge it immediately. I could write a wish and entertain it or be a calm parent to a child mid-tantrum. I could be petty, wild, and free. Those pages were – and continue to be – a lifeline for me. I can explore all the parts of me that I otherwise kept hidden or didn't know how to speak about with my parents, friends, or partner.

I'm able to explore my inner world.

When I was a senior in college, some friends and I took shrooms. I'd pressed my fingers into the plastic baggy, pulling out the dried plant, and sprinkled it onto a piece of toast. Crunching, teeth working, taste buds angry from the bitterness, I swallowed them down.

As soon as I said, "I don't feel anything," the room began to glisten. The sun slipped inside the windowpanes to dance on the once white walls, each ray an ice skater in a sparkled rainbow leotard. My mind breathed that afternoon, a set of lungs expanding and contracting. We put our feet into a warm bubble bath and my eyes could feel the warmth and my feet could see their reflection.

At one point, I stood in front of a mirror. There I was, barely 21, both feet on the ground and a 120 pounds of flesh, completely unattached from any past part of myself. Standing in front of the looking glass, I watched myself age.

The skin on my face wrinkled and creased. My eyes sunk and the lines surrounding them celebrated years of expression. My hair spun a silver purple as soft threads escaped my ears and feathered the nape of my neck. Transfixed, I remained at that mirror for an unknown amount of time, watching elastic skin and energized eyes shape shift into a weathered, wrinkled face that was home to pupils so deep, so wise. She nodded at me, and I nodded back.

I'm going to have a long life. The knowing shot through my youth-full veins, pulling my shoulders back, and planting my feet more firmly onto the bathroom tiles. *I am here for a good long while.*

Many folks who have consumed mushrooms have spoken about their spiritual connection to the divine, to something greater than themselves. (There is evidence aplenty for how this sacred plant promotes mental healing, so I won't be the one to rehash that here.) I was awash with a brilliancy I had never quite felt before that moment. The message I got, at twenty-one years old, was that there was nothing to cling onto, not even life. It all unfolds as it needs to. I was here, I would grow old, and I would experience everything I needed to in this walkabout on Earth. I could relax into it, allow it to unfold.

This mindset shows me the way, even today as I write this chapter during a Midwest spring. Looking out onto my Minnesota lawn, I watch as the clovers quiver from droplets of midnight rain, untouched by the sensation of the sun. I can depend on change, as the day will rise and fall; every experience I am meant to have will arrive and depart. I get to trust my part in it all.

I wasn't just in Colorado to prepare for and run a race. I was there because it was part of my grand unfolding. In this moment, I followed my bliss, my desires, and the doors began to open, with a steady, well-oiled ease: an opportunity with the Life Time Foundation, the house in Alma, the truck driver and his shovel, Colleen's steady guidance up the road. Once I made the decision to leave for Colorado and surrendered to it, everything began to operate like gears in a Swiss watch.

I'm here for a good long while, I wrote with hands that reminded me of my mother's.

I trust that it will all work out, I underlined.

There is something bigger than me at work here, written as the woman I knew I was becoming.

* * *

The cabin was expansive. Not so much in size, but in how I felt within it. Tall windows brought in morning light and the mountains revealed themselves, as though slipping a lunar nightgown off their shoulders at sunrise.

Over the first few weeks, my routine began to take shape.

Moving softly through the home so as not to disturb my three roommates, seasonal workers in Colorado in the ski and snowboard scene. I brewed coffee and grabbed a protein bar as my "first breakfast." I shook up an Athletic Greens shake as the coffee brewed and sipped it as I lightly stretched my cranky body into being. Once I was ready for caffeine, I poured a mug and, in those earlier days of April, made a fire in the wood stove as the coffee steamed. Wrapping myself in a blanket, I plunked on the well-worn couch, cracked open my notebook, and began writing my three morning pages.

Meditation has never come easily for me. I am sure many of us can agree. Yet, I tried my best to take every opportunity I could to prepare my mind to meet my body for the challenge of a hundred miles. I couldn't fathom a summer of mountain training without some sort of meditation practice to still my mind, stretch the muscles of focus, and encourage new neuron pathways to develop to work in my favor. I didn't want to just practice mindfulness while my feet were in motion over a winding alpine trail. I wanted to gear up my psyche with mental training well before the miles were run by meditating with my butt on a cushion.

Many mornings, this took the form of a guided meditation through my favored app, Insight Timer. Sometimes I selected a 10-20 minute guided session; other times, a sound bath or binaural beats. This would aid me tremendously in getting through big, chunky mileage during the next few months. Later, during runs, I would listen to similar tracks.

As I sat on the couch in the early hours of the day, the cabin creaked its way to life. Typically emerging first from the bedrooms below the main floor was Tucker. Soft spoken and sweet, he was an arborist in the summer and delivery driver for Door Dash in the winter. He poured coffee to go, smiled a good morning at me, and then, stuffing his boots onto his feet, was out the door.

The other two roommates would rise not long after Tucker

left. During the winter months, they worked at a local resort. Caroline was an admin and her boyfriend Zach a ski instructor. During the summer months, they navigated job changes, taking on work that both suited the season and their desire to get out on mountain bikes whenever possible. At their side was an overweight Blue Healer who barked at her own shadow. Once they awoke, the air fryer sizzled on and hash browns were tossed into the heat. Eggs and bacon followed. The aromas wafting from the kitchen was usually my cue to get ready for my day.

During the late afternoon, after my virtual coaching work was done, I got into the car and rolled a couple thousand feet in altitude down the mountain toward the towns of Breckenridge and Frisco. There, I was able to breathe a bit easier. The first few weeks, I did not run; instead, I hiked, walked, and slowly got accustomed to the thin air.

This was a helpful starting place for my body. In fact, it was all that my run coach, Greg, had requested of me and realistically all I could do in those first couple weeks. Headphones on, I listened to podcasts, with Rich Roll, Sally McRae, David Roche, and Glennon Doyle. I took steps and breaths. Step step. Breath, breath.

As I walked, I watched my breath turn into a foggy puff in front of my face, small clouds of exhaled water meeting the cool blue air of the ski town. Those first few walks taught me to look up and outward, to take notice of and take in my surroundings without worrying about pace or mileage or how my body felt. No analyzing workout data or keeping a certain pace or holding back to maintain my heart rate (That would all come soon in my training.) All I needed to do was acclimate, slow and steady. The tough days would arrive soon enough.

In a few weeks, I began to sleep better, and I was finally ready to begin the next big phase of ultra training.

* * *

The summer was filled with space between the moments I got to run. There was a vast playground of trails, and I wanted to see as many of them as I could. The weekends were completely open for me to find a trail, pack up my nutrition, trekking poles, and hydration pack and set out for hours of solo time on my feet.

I ran through trails in neighboring towns, including Buena Vista, Fairplay, Frisco and Breckenridge. I explored alone and with new friends I made from the Breckenridge run club. I even dog sat a mountain dog named Freya, embarking on long lonely miles and returning to snuggle her in a hot heap on the couch. I chose to wake up each day to move my body purposefully, holding the goal of Leadville and the purpose of the Life Time Foundation as lighthouses in the mind, steering me back to a gentle shore.

A few times, I made my way out to the course, running Turquoise Lake, Powerline, and even double Hope Pass (twice). These trips built a necessary confidence in me. A confidence that is only created from experience. My body got stronger each time I hit the trails on the course and my mind followed suit.

Running has slowly become more meditative than competitive; I wrote in my journal mid-summer. *The gentle and rhythmic slap of shoes against dirt, the attention to inhaling and exhaling, and the ways I have to let go of my thoughts. I can be with myself. Like, really BE with myself.*

The scrawl in my composition notebook was big, bold, and confident: *I'm finding a safe place in my body all over again.*

My body had not always felt like a safe place — not when fear imprinted itself in childhood, not when old beliefs clung tight. But, Ben had nudged me forward. Chris had held me, and Leadville had opened its arms up for me to arrive within. The hypnosis session had cracked a window. And now, the mountain air was rushing through.

24

Unlearning

The deepest wound
I carry
is the one
titled,
"You aren't important."
I'm trying
to hold her
(little me)
in ways
that say,
"I love you"
and
"You matter here"
but
unlearned words
take so long
to make
a memory.
I keep

trying,
building
a sanctuary
unknown to me.
I look in the mirror
I squeeze myself tight.
I stay at it
again and again:
"I love you."
and
"You matter here."
I keep at it,
unlearning
the unnecessary
lessons
of un–importance.

25

The Day I Left My Body

12 years (or so) before Race Day

The following chapter recounts moments where I did not give consent, an important part of my story to Leadville. Please read with tenderness and awareness of how these stories may impact you. As always, please seek support as needed and remember —
you are stronger than you know.

"No, no!" I thought I was shouting but it surfaced as a soft, scared moan, "Just beso, beso!" An attractive Puerto Rican man was on top of me in my resort room, pressing hard against my shorts and tugging at their sides. I just wanted to be kissed. I did not want where this was leading.

I was twenty and we met the evening before this encounter while my older brother and I were exploring Puerto Rico to celebrate his graduation from a master's program. My brother and I met new friends on the beach and, before we knew it, we were all out dancing. An impeccable host, one of the men linked our arms, carrying us into a night of tropical haze. He and I locked eyes, and as soon as my brother was lost in the sea of hot skin and bare feet, I kissed the man (or he kissed me). When the club began to close down, I was nestled in his arms.

My body was fluid and happy, a magical riptide of warm breeze, gentle touch, and buzzing newness. I liked his attention on me and I liked how I felt impossibly beautiful in his eyes. My runner's legs shone tan against a bright yellow sundress that night and I had a strangers arms wrapped around my hips. I felt safe, happy.

The next day, he arrived at our resort to spend more time with us. All three of us enjoyed rum and cokes poolside, the unrelenting June sun bursting through patchy island clouds. My brother leaned back on the poolside bar stool, a goofy grin encasing his face as the celebratory drinks took a pleasant hold. There was no reason to be anything but carefree; I felt it, too. Partway through the early afternoon, I needed to run up to the resort room to brush out my tangled chlorine hair. Without a word, the man joined me, guiding me up the elevator with a hand on my low back.

I couldn't speak much Spanish, and his English was broken. We had mainly communicated through our bodies the last two days: hand holding, hugs, enormous smiles and flirtatious touches. Every motion was innocent and gentle as we both had the awareness of my brother nearby us. Up in the hotel room was the first time I was truly alone with him. And sometime between the door closing in the resort room and me reaching for my hairbrush, he pressed himself on top of me on one of the queen beds. I was pinned down and I did not like it, did not want it.

I could feel the enormous flooding of stress through my nervous system, activating all the alarms I had internally. My hands, speaking for me since my words could not, tried to press him away.

I no longer felt safe. I was not safe.

"Si, si," he cooed back and within seconds I felt his naked heat at the side of my shorts. Everything inside of me froze. All the alarm systems in my body seemed to cease. The sun streamed in the room, revealing a normal day with broad daylight hues, noticing everything, highlighting it all. Dark strains of my scarlet anger slipped through the AC vent as shame whispered with spit and spiced breath in my ear, *Look at what you made him do.*

My body is not my own, I thought.

Or maybe I just felt it.

My hands dropped from his chest. I lay still. I stared up at the ceiling.

"No…" another whisper, unheard or ignored.

Doesn't matter which. He did not listen and pressed himself all the way inside of me.

That's the day I left my body.

I slipped out of her, like a pair of worn pants to the floor. My spirit drifted toward the ceiling fan and stayed there. I watched as he pulled out of me, how my one tear never turned into two. I watched as he buttoned up, smiled, put his arm around me as I go off the bed, and guided me out the hotel room down the elevator toward more rum by the pool.

I watched my body learn how to move through the world to shield pain. I watched as the little girl in that body shrank away, horrified and scared.

When this happened, I was barely out of my teens.

No one was there to tell me, "I love you; I'm sorry." No one felt right for me to tell this to anyway. I turned into a silent, secretive young woman, making a space so large inside of me it could hold this man's behavior as my own. But that space pressed me from the inside out, forcing my spirit to the side.

When I returned to college that fall, running became foreign to me. I didn't want to know anything about the body I was in and was left watching it from afar, in a long-distance relationship to her, numbed and disengaged.

It would be a decade before I could speak this story aloud and get the deep listening, hand holding, and therapeutic healing that I needed, including a somatic therapist specializing in trauma. Like many wounds, however, scar tissue remains. Those scars, and the echoes of my childhood, followed me in my body to

Leadville.

* * *

It happened again by a college friend.

Like a drunk gentleman, he escorted me to my dorm after a party. However, I woke up in a fog, the clock on the wall ticking toward 4 a.m., to him inside of me, fully awake and moving his hips. Without my consent. Without me knowing. My mind slurred along with my words from a night of partying as I pulled away and said, "Stop."

Did I ask him to? Did I suggest we hook up? I wasn't entirely sure; I just knew that it didn't feel right.

The next day, I attempted to tell my then-boyfriend, avoiding the "R" word so as not to spook him, or me. He became angry and called me a "slut." The shame magnified. I went to talk to security and the campus police had me answer a million questions. The men there told me to not drink, wear decent clothing, and be safe.

Safe. I wasn't safe in my own body.

I felt dirty and exposed, unsure of where to go. A complicated mess lurked inside me; it felt as though my organs were being rearranged each time. I grew an increasing sense that I couldn't possibly deserve love, and that turned into me believing I didn't deserve to feel happiness and success. That there was too much wrong with me and the skin I was in. *My body is a sin.* Guilt and shame from years of Catholic upbringing banged their fists in my chest, again and again.

I became foolish and risky in my behavior with men after that. Due to an injury (both physical of a fractured knee and this psychological one), I wasn't able to perform on the cross country and track team at the high level I was accustomed to. Instead, I drank. I danced on table tops and lost my way through campus on unsteady high heels. Boys grabbed me anywhere they liked and I let them.

I abandoned my self. And I sought love from all the wrong places.

I dated the same person on and off and on and off again, crying and begging for him to love me the way I needed. He was the same boyfriend who had called me a slut. I didn't know anymore what I needed; it was too foreign. How could I make room for a good love when there was so much shame pulsing through me? I had left the front door of my self locked and shuttered each window tightly. No love could fully get in.

I got good at stuffing down the pain. A numbness broke in, stretching out its legs, pulling off its wide tongued boots — and plopped down to stay. Running then became an escape from feeling instead of a retreat to a feeling. I could block out my emotional grief by physically hurting. My twenties thrust me from place to place, run to run, race to race, relationship to relationship. Aching to be loved. Pushing my body to the extremes in order not to feel something.

But how can a body that has not belonged to herself get the care she desperately needs? The years turned, wayward and wild. Yet, running remained at my side.

As a high school freshman, I had zoomed around a track for the first time, feeling a strength that's potential I could not yet harness. I discovered that running could take me out of the house, away from Catholicism, and into a new kind of magical world all of my own. A world where I felt significant. A world where I was in charge of my body, my mind, my feelings, and in control. A world that tumbled after those moments in college. I lost hold of the scaffolding, and the foundation cracked beneath me.

For years, I was lost in my own body. For years, I forgot what true strength felt like. It wasn't until my thirties, more than a decade later, that I could come back home to myself. I took the shutters down, I opened the closets and looked under the bed. I swept and tended to the rooms within me.

Reclaiming through time, spaciousness, and adventure. Seeing what my body was — and was not. Not a body for the Church. Not a body for the men who took it. Not a body for an unknown, future husband. I was reclaiming a body that was my own, in a place I chose to strengthen it, in ways that delighted me.

In that Alma cabin up at altitude, training for the Leadville 100, I was now remodeling and decorating.

I spent a lot of time on my own, heading out into Summit County to find another trail, carrying my phone with the

All-Trails app and the map pre-downloaded. Sometimes, depending on the location, I carried bear spray and a small pocketknife. Patting my pack every few miles to feel their shape, I reassured myself: I was safe. I was safe. I was safe.

I set out for entire afternoons, my blood pumping, legs stretching out over the trail, ponytail flopping at the top of my head, a clear mind beneath it. I could be a new kind of free here. I could have autonomy. I could surrender my body to the act of running and somehow feel like I mattered, like it all could make sense.

From time to time, I met with local runners for quality miles and good conversation. The Breckenridge Running Club was my main mode of connection. I discovered their page scrolling through Facebook in my early weeks in Alma. It wasn't long before I met with Susan, the established Masters Marathoner, who took me onto the stretching vastness of the Colorado Trail around Breckenridge. And then I met Cindi, the chatty and vibrant Final Descents runner who had conquered cancer over the years and was training for the Leadville 100 alongside me. Then Tracy, who was a seasoned ultra marathoner followed by Don, the treadmill world record holder and Cody, the owner of America's Highest Gym in Alma. I was surrounded by good people who knew me plainly as a strong runner.

Although those connections were gold – with running companions offering me insight on how to approach the mountains, what to expect in an ultra marathon, how to dress for unpredictable weather patterns, and helping me maintain a steady "talking pace," – I preferred to run alone, creating a deeper well of security and confidence within myself. A well that I could dip into and drink from anytime I pleased. Step by step on the alpine trails, sip by sip of security.

Every mile a reminder that this is what safety feels like in all creases, crevasses, and corners of myself. Sacred breathing from my solar plexus, steady rhythm in my heart, swing of strength in my arms.

Like a leaf making its way down a steady river toward a great sea, I began to find my way back to my self. I began to feel safe in the skin I was in. I felt like that young, freshman runner in her track uniform, full of life and love for the sport — and a new love for my body. The rustle of the trees cheered me on, and the audible throb of summer's insects soothed me through every dusty mile.

Notice thoughts. Speak to yourself with compassion. Embody the change. Mantras that followed me from the ultra runner up and into the Rocky Mountain wilderness. *I am worthy. I am mighty. I am everything I need to be.*

In Alma, April turned to May. Then, June dependably arrived. I got my mind and body ready to run a few important races on my way to the Leadville 100: The Leadville Trail Marathon, Ragnar Trail Colorado in Snowmass, and the Silver Rush 50.

I am mighty. I am everything I need to be. I reminded myself each day.

26

We Are the Mighty Mountain

I painted for an hour
when my mind would not sit still.
Every little brushstroke
brought me flow up until
the thunder started rolling
lightning slashed the sky
so, I wandered to the kitchen
cup of coffee, slice of pie
to look out beyond the fir trees
at the mountain standing tall—
I wondered if it mattered
my mind couldn't relax at all.
Then I felt the mountain
rising in my bones
I realized every thought was like
alpine wind that's blown
sweeping noise inside me
kicking up what's there:
rain and sleet and hail

storming icy air.
But peaks don't bother changing
the brilliance that they are
just because the weather strikes
or leaves behind a scar.
So I bit into my pastry
with my brow turned to the sky—
We are a mighty mountain.
Our thoughts: weather passing by.

27

My Body Belongs to Me

The Leadville 100: Approaching Outward Bound Aid Station at
23.5 miles

I barreled down the other side of Sugarloaf Pass, affectionately known as Powerline. The sun was awake now, as was my body. Miles before, I had let the handkerchief fall from my nose. The heat was beginning to creep into the air and the trees all seemed strong, powerful, applauding me as I passed by.

The force of gravity pulled me down the zigzagged dirt trail in long, loping strides. Without thinking—more a guttural urge—I whooped with a frenzy. Someone echoed behind me. My lips exaggerated upward, tongue out, nose scrunched with pleasure. Hell yeah.

There's an invincibility in the air that only the first quarter of an ultra marathon in the mountains can offer. The biggest challenges hadn't yet emerged, and the power of a strong taper and enthused start pressed us forward.

Earlier, I had arrived at the first aid station, Mayqueen, with a pep in my step. After traversing Turquoise Lake, sidestepping roots and watching every step, I reminded myself to "keep slow and steady." It was part of my race strategy not to stop there. Instead, I pulled out a gel, sucked it down, and moved on.

Love it, I thought watching the swirl of runners slow to accept help in the form of paper cups and gel packets. *Don't need it.* Onward I shuffled—ten more miles to Outward Bound.

Clicking down the Powerline descent, whooping and galloping like a herd of horses, we emerged onto pavement. This stretch held the grandest amount of road on the entire course, leading to Outward Bound before curving off again toward the trails.

I settled onto the side of the road, whispering to my legs, *Carry me easy.* They ignored me. I churned forward, dropping the fastest miles of the day.

Whoops.

I knew Chris was planning to meet me at the big field. We didn't know what to expect, other than it would be crowded. Like a beehive in a Colorado blue spruce, I heard the buzz of people before I saw them. Cheers erupted for runners around me. I turned right toward the open field—volunteer tents on one side, a throng of spectators on the other. Shouts, music, dogs barking, KT tape ripping.

But no Chris.

I slowed to a walk, scanning the crowd for his familiar flannel shirt. I was hungry, ready for the peanut butter bagel he was supposed to have for me.

Nothing.

I pivoted to Plan B. I'd prepped drop bags for a few stations, including this one. I asked a volunteer for mine. He returned with the clear plastic bag dotted with the butterfly stickers I'd placed there with excitement a few days prior. Distracted and thrown due to missing Chris, I enlisted the volunteer to help me.

"What do you need?" he asked, on the ready to be both a lending hand and emotional support.

"I need water in these." I handed over my bottles, allowing my mind to settle from the churn of looking for Chris.

I opened the drop bag and pulled out a smaller baggie of white powder—my high-calorie nutrition. Normally, you fill a bottle halfway with water, add the powder, shake, then top it off. I knew this. I'd practiced this, I knew this. But, I was distracted. The bottles were already full, and I just dumped the powder onto the top and shook.

Then, I stuffed them back into my pack and took off.

Sticky hands. No support from Chris. The sun rising. The miles stretched ahead.

About a half mile out, I tried to drink. Nothing. The powder clogged the valves. Annoyed, I tried again. Still nothing. I sighed, realizing I'd have to rely on the gels and back bladder.

As if summoned by mosquitoes, frustration bit at me. No Chris. No peanut butter bagel. Clogged bottles. All of it stacked—each a mosquito, and now I was swarmed.

I needed a mental reset.

I pulled out my headphones and hit shuffle.

Atmosphere came on, a Minneapolis artist who I loved. The song: "Best Day."

I laughed as I listened to the lyrics. They were explicitly telling me that every day couldn't possibly be the best. It went on to instruct me to just do what I could.

Fine. Doing what I can, I thought. Just because I missed Chris and botched my bottles didn't mean the race was over. Not by a long shot.

Then my phone buzzed. It was Chris calling and because there was service on that part of the course, he was able to reach me. He was at Outward Bound, looking for me, but I was already almost a mile past! We missed each other in the crowd and he thought I hadn't yet arrived. Relief passed between us before we hung up: he knew I was safe and I knew he didn't miss me on purpose.

145

I kept moving. Me and my strong body. We pushed on.

Running offers so much: time to yourself, stillness of mind, nature's embrace, freedom, and decisions that make your body feel more like your own.

If I could bottle this, I would. The label would read: "Become more connected, grounded, and resilient. Your body belongs to YOU."

Because truthfully, my body never felt like mine.

As a child, strangers touched my hair and cheeks while my parents encouraged politeness. I learned not to say no. Priests pulled me onto laps. If I objected, I was rude. Naughty. Sent to my room.I learned women's bodies weren't their own, but tools for others' comfort and pleasure.

At eight, I joined my father at the March for Life in Washington, DC. Posters of bloodied embryos filled the sky and I remember hating all the women who chose to abort their babies. I swore to myself that I would never let my selfishness push me toward such a choice. That shape shifted into internalized shame over the years, a buried belief that a woman could not make a decision for herself about her body.

As a teen, I became aware of my changing body. My father's booming voice once declared, "Go put a shirt on; it's like looking down the Grand Canyon!" after I bent over to zip my backpack. Later, after practice, he scolded, "Your nipples are showing through your sports bra. That's disrespectful to your coach. Go change."

Mortified. Compliant. Again, and again.

This body, I learned, was shameful. Not mine.

In high school and college, I rebelled. I craved unconditional love and bodily autonomy, but lacked the tools to build it. Instead, I sought validation through appearances, through men.

I remember one summer day as a young teenager, walking with two of my sisters down our dead end street alongside the local golf course. Ponytails swishing, shorts riding high, we showed off as much skin as we could. We laughed and leaned close, strutting. Every car that drove by, we flirtatiously waved at, hoping for a man to beep his horn and show us that our bodies were worthy. The farmhouse door of my parent's house had closed on the expectation that we were to be covered up and keep to ourselves. Out here, in the sunshine, we thought we controlled our bodies and all the gazes that were drawn to us. Looking back, I want to hug those girls, let them know that car horns and men's gazes were not an indication of worth.

That kind of worthiness was shallow. But, I didn't know it then; I didn't have an understanding of what the term "male gaze" even meant. All I knew was that I felt powerful in some way because men noticed me. And, in turn, it made me feel more worthy in my body.

Leadville — and every ultra running experience of mine — was the evolved, healthier form of this power. This time, I was showing up for no one but myself. I had an opportunity for true embodiment in a body that deeply belonged to me.

This time, my body was mine. This time, my body was an incredible instrument, not a decorated object, not overtaken by a man, not instructed who or how to be. Ponytail swishing and all, this body was truly my own. My body belongs to me.

Running has helped me shed shame over the years. On the track, in the woods, on trails—I felt powerful. My coaches noticed my grit. My teammates saw my strength. I worked hard. I laughed. I ran. And I kept healing something mighty inside of myself. Sometimes I wonder who I'd be without running. But more than that—I know who I became because of it.

I fell into step with another woman and together we took the power of our bodies into the forest toward more climbing and more technical trails.

28

Prediction

On the moonlit beach I saw her:
the woman I'll grow to be —
barefoot in a simple dress
speaking poems down by the sea.
I thought that she might notice
as I waved my hand her way
but she was busy catching shooting stars,
eyes sparkling with play.
Her hair was swept into a bun
with wisps dancing by her ears,
her jaw and brow were joined just so
with joy lines from the years.
Her arms rose to hug her shoulders
as she walked along the tide–
there was an ease in her body
a quiet power in her stride.
I sat and marveled at her,
amazed at the future me:
a content and mighty drifter

speaking poems down by the sea.

29

Race Reports and Journal Entries

June and July before Race Day

I signed up for a couple key races as training runs. Each one arrived with a tumble, and I somersaulted right in.

My ultra running coach, Greg, organized training around each of these races to test my legs, mind, nutrition, altitude acclimation, and, of course—endurance. I planned weekends around these trials not only for physical conditioning but also for joy. My guiding principle: Arrive at the start line happy and healthy. That was my goal for each race—and for Leadville, too.

My first event was the Leadville Marathon. Just a few months earlier in January, I'd imagined June to have warm, perfect, bluebird skies. But you cannot trust the mountain to behave. Instead, you bank on it teasing you with sunshine, then turning on you the moment you get comfortable. That's exactly what happened.

The night before the race, I met up with a crew of other racers—Cindi, Alex, and Lisa—at a campground just a few kilometers from the start line. As I rumbled up the road, butterflies ignited in my belly. My first ever mountain race, with people I didn't know, in a new place, car camping for the first time, and with the biggest goal in mind yet.

Turning off the ignition, I paused. Breathe, Barbara. This is all part of the magic. This is it.

I climbed out of my Subaru, hoodie pulled tight, water bottle in hand. A waving hand reached out the window of an idling SUV parked at the campsite, welcoming me in. Within seconds, I was reminded how special the trail running community is—bonded by a shared love of movement and mud. Alex, Lisa, and Cindi were huddled together inside the car to stay dry from the rainfall and immediately made me feel like part of the crew after mere moments of chit chat.

The night stayed wet. I cocooned in my own car, wrapped in layers and a sleeping bag. I'd never been car camping before and didn't expect it to get so frigid! When my alarm went off before sunrise, my windows were a frosted reminder of how low the temperature must have dipped — must have been in the low 30s. Shivering, I started the engine, peeled off layers, got dressed, and made my way to the main campsite.

Alex and Lisa were already there, chatting over a steaming pot of hot water. I added instant coffee to a mug and joined them. Within the hour, we piled into Cindi's car, chattering about the weather and the course. Snow, rain, and—maybe, just maybe—

sunshine.

Lisa began to sing: *"I got sunshine on a cloudy day..."*

We joined her: *"When it's cold outside, I got the month of May..."*

Then we belted out together: *"I guess you'd say, what could make me feel this way? LEADVILLE! Talking 'bout Leadville... LEADVILLE!"*

We were ready to take on the Rocky Mountain trails.

Race Report: Leadville Marathon

For race day, I opted for my bike-length shorts, long compression socks, a tank, neon half-zip, and a rain jacket. I stuffed my Osprey pack (1.5L) with 4 Huma gels, 2 Glukose packs, a Cliff Bar, and 2 electrolyte salt tabs. I ate it all, plus potato chips and a swig of Coke at the (almost) top of Mosquito Pass. Because of the year's heavy snowfall, the race director forced a course reroute just below the summit—so we didn't quite hit the true high point, but the effort felt just as steep and raw. Even with the adjustment, we still covered over 26.2 miles with roughly 6,000 feet of elevation gain—most of it on rugged, historic mining roads and rocky single track.

Took a few miles to warm up, but I felt ease power hiking the climbs. I'm becoming a stronger downhill runner, too. Weather was wild—wet snow, hail-like slush, and slippery mud, true to Leadville form. The course winds through sections of the Mineral Belt Trail, Ball Mountain, and California Gulch, all steeped in Leadville's mining history and elevation-laced brutality. I chatted with a few dudes on the course, but mostly stayed in my own head, heart, and body. Not a full-out effort, more like 75%. I finished as the 22nd woman overall out of about 200 women, a solid effort on a trialing terrain, with a finishing time of 5:21.

I also tweaked my ankle around mile twenty-one but shook it out. (An icy creek back at camp afterward worked as a recovery bath.) They announced my name at the finish line, which always feels special and meaningful, a happy punctuation mark on a tiring morning. Afterward, I huddled around a heater with a beer and cheered on the other runners.

Cindi, Alex, Lisa, and I tried to go to Mountain Pies, but the wait was too long. So we headed to Buena Vista instead— fifteen degrees warmer and sunny. Spent another cold night car camping.

Then next day, Cindi and I ran sixteen miles from our campsite near Leadville. My left foot was still tender, but I managed. I ran out of water with a few miles to go and fortunately Cindi shared her pack with me. Once back in Alma, I slept a restful, wonderful eight hours.

This race felt like a hazy dream. Did we really just do that? Did I just get to experience a taste of what Leadville is all about?

Race Report: Trail Ragnar Colorado in Snowmass

After a weekend adventure in Snowmass Colorado (right by

Aspen) I am back home in Alma. Nibbling a protein bagel with peanut butter and sipping coffee and still feeling the pulse from the Trail Ragnar weekend. I ended up running an extra loop – we had a team of eight, and everyone was assigned 3 loops. However, a teammate faced shock due to the cold and the trails (she hadn't quite done anything like this before) and she had to go to the ER in the middle of the night. Another teammate took her, leaving both of their early morning loops without a runner. So, at 5 a.m., I got myself out of my warm-ish sleeping bag and tent in the not-so-warm, frosty morning and bundled up to do the green loop. Three and a half miles with two of those steady climbing. The trails took me right up to the ridge line where I could overlook Snowmass Village beneath the glow of sunrise. All the birds came out with me – singing and chattering, preparing for the day. Magnificent wildflowers everywhere you could look. Yellows and purples, sunshine and mountain majesty.

Trail Ragnars are long, exhausting, and incredible affairs. Our "home base" was a campsite with two 4-person tents and an adjoining canopy tent. Beneath was a wagon filled with our food and snacks. A cot to catch snoozes on, stretch on, get ready to run on. Trash bag to collect wrappers and what not. Camp chairs in a semi-circle where the team sat and chatted and learned about each other.

We were called The Tuff Tatas. I was the "mountain goat," taking on extra miles for training. Lisa, our captain and a breast cancer survivor, radiated joy and knew everything about credit card points. Brianna, a small but mighty army nurse, dubbed me "mountain goat." Naomi, an engineer and triathlete,

155

breathed the wild. Ann, a ball of mom-energy. Stephanie, the comedian, hoarse and drinking White Claw out of a Nalgene. Laura, quiet and peaceful. Alexis, sweet and spontaneous, the one who ended up in the ER.

I was the eighth and last runner. The day started (Friday) with Brianna taking off on the green loop and then went Laura, the Stephanie, Alexis then Naomi, Anne, Lisa, and finally me. I did the yellow first. 4.4 miles that gave a series of switchbacks and offered a fun, loping mountain bike path downhill where I could really open up my legs and go. My second leg was around 1:30 a.m., the green loop at three and a half miles. I was steady eddy going up in the dark; my headlamp worked well enough and fits just fine on my hat. It was a thrill to run in the middle of the night, albeit cold when I was just standing around waiting to go. Great training for Leadville.

Two hours later, I was running the same loop again for Alexis. I got to rest up for a while after, enjoy the morning and my teammates, snack and sip on coffee before going out on the red loop and my favorite of the three. That 6.6 miles brought me 1000 feet up before the delicious reward of 1000 feet down! I really am getting more skilled at downhill running and can feel my quads growing in much-needed strength. I'll need that for the Leadville 100.

Journal Entry: June 23, 8:12 AM

I've been in Colorado over two months. Something is stirring in me. Restless. The cabin is holding something—or I am. Yesterday I bought crystals: selenite for the doorways, tourmaline for protection, and mahogany obsidian "to strengthen the aura." Noah at the shop was lovely.

Chris got his ticket to visit in July for Silver Rush 50. I get to share this with him. He gives me space. I give it back. Maybe we'll make it. Maybe we'll be okay.

My sister Sarah has called a lot lately. We talk about womanhood. The expectation to be sweet, never sour; nurturing, never sexy. But I am all of it. I'm sour and hot and wild and alive. I promise to keep exploring what it means to be a woman. To hold sacred the divine feminine.

My body is wondrous. She senses, absorbs, plays, and speaks. Beauty. Strength. Desire. Pleasure. All my own. No one else. All the goodness I want to feel toward myself—I already have inside of me.

And when I run, I seem to remember this. It's almost like a kind of prayer, but not like the ones from the rosary beads in childhood. These footsteps of mine are quiet, steady, and real. The trail doesn't ask me to be anything but exactly who I am. There's no push for me to behave or sit still or be ladylike. Instead, it gives me all the space for everything else! I have the spaciousness to be wild, move as I please, and reject anything that demands perfection from me.

Just the other day, I was in Buena Vista on a new-to-me trail. There weren't other hikers or dog walkers or runners around and at times I felt like I was being watched. The sensation scared me so much, I began to envision a mountain lion stalking

157

me. I had to take a few deep breaths, remind myself that I was
shit-out-of-luck anyway if an animal was stalking me, and I
just put a foot in front of the other to run.

When I run, I can hear myself more clearly. There's something
sacred about showing up for the hard parts and choosing to
keep going even when it hurts a little or you're unsure of what
might happen next. You choose to come back to yourself, to
come home to your body. Maybe that's what real growth is.
Not some big firework moment, but instead a quiet kind of
returning. Over and over again.

I think the little girl in me is mighty proud of who the adult
Barbara is becoming.

Race Report: Silver Rush 50

Back in Leadville. This time, Chris was town visiting. The first
thing he did was wash my filthy car, which by that point had
seen many miles of dusty front range roads. By the time we got
to the tube hill for a 6 a.m. start, I was energized and ready to
go; however, Chris was hit hard by the oxygen deprivation
which, understandably, made him a little grumpy. He was
physically there, but also so much more uncomfortable than
me. I gave him as much love as I could, but I needed to hone in
on what would fuel me for the big day ahead. I zeroed in on the
happenings around me and allowed myself to get pulled by the
inescapable, positive frenzy.

The race began straight up the tubing hill, named for all the
sledding I'm sure that's done there over the wintertime! The

first man and woman to the top get an entry into the Leadville 100, meaning some folks started the race in a dead sprint uphill. Not me; I power hiked to the top and then let gravity pull me into the wooded trails that followed.

Ultimately, it was a pretty great training day and I collected over 7,000 feet of elevation gain over forty-eight miles. I felt incredible for the majority of this race. There were lots of hiking and technical rocky sections, as well as plenty of long loping downhills. It warmed up something fierce; by the second half, the course was a scorcher on the exposed trails and dirt Jeep roads. It became essential to drink my fluids and refill at each aid station, and continue to get calories in me every 20-30 minutes. But by the time I was within earshot of the finish line — about two miles yet! — I had stopped eating and was pressing forward in a walk/jog as best I could. Somewhere on the course a woman on the sidelines shouted out to me, "You're the next big thing!" Because of her — and maybe some delusional belief in her words — I mentally survived this one.

I went into this race hoping for a top-fifteen finish for women, yet I got sixteenth with a time of 9:49. The last few miles were a slog as the heat, sun exposure, and lowered calorie intake settled in. With a tired mind, I slowed and let two women passed me. Ah well — I am super happy with the effort. I mostly fueled well, but wish I'd had more "real" food as I depended quite a bit on gels.

My coach, Greg, wrote into my training to get a marathon completed the next day, which would be the biggest double effort of my summer. As the athlete, I also had an opportunity to go with my gut and make a decision on what would be better for my mind and body. I compromised with Greg. Instead of the full marathon, I would get some kind of double digit run done, but do so mere hours after the completion of the fifty miler. That meant an opportunity to get night running experience, along with the massive buildup of fatigue that comes from being in a race.

Chris and I pitched a tent at our Leadville campsite with Cindi. I set my alarm for 3 a.m. When it tinkled, Chris stirred slightly, waking up just enough to tell me to be careful and kiss me good luck. Cindi plodded over to our site with her headlamp and in a fit of delirious giggles — what were we doing! What followed was eleven miles of slow and steady movement from the trails onto the road headed toward Powerline, Mount Massive keeping dark watch in the night. For the first real time, I felt what it was like to keep my body moving in the midst of gripping fatigue and a complete desire to curl back under the blankets with my lover. Instead of sleeping, we slipped cold banana into our mouths and sidestepped rocks that appeared out of nowhere.

Our watches beeped for the eighth mile split. "Turn off your headlamp," Cindi stage whispered to me. I didn't ask why she was whispering with no one within miles of us, nor did I ask why she wanted our lamps out. I simply obeyed.

And then, we looked up.

Later, I would learn I was looking at what is called a "Scorpion star party." With twinkling, magical streaking that van Gogh would approve, stars swept across the rich, black sky. We could even see Mars, a soft red positioned beside a brilliant peppering of white. We didn't move for many minutes. I'm not sure we were even breathing. We were frozen in the undeniable cellular experience of awe.

I bottled up that emotion for safe keeping in my own inner apothecary. I hope to always carry it with me throughout the rest of my training — and my life.

30

Crushing It

The Leadville 100: Twin Lakes Aid Station Outbound, 38 miles

I was crying while sputtering, "You guys are amazing, I am so happy to see you!"

Chris knelt in front me, my right foot in one hand and a pocket knife in the other, gently stabbing at a blister on my toe. My eyes filled. I was overwhelmed. Next to him stood Cindi, guiding me to choose between the sugary, savory, or hydrating options on the table beside us. Hallie was all smiles behind them, taking a photo with an intense I'm-so-proud-of-you smile. Trapper, my pacer for late in the race, stood at attention at the front of the tent, already gearing up for his pacing duties in many an hour. Don, the local ultra runner who had given me good advice going into the race, was in his element, arms crossed against a Hawaiian shirt beside Trapper. I was at mile 38, about to head into my climb up Hope Pass to over 12,000 feet, and I was in a pink cloud of achy ultra running joy.

Moments ago, I was zigzagging my way down mini Mt Elbert. The gravel, stones, and dirt of the Jeep road made it a potentially treacherous downhill. My quads were beginning to sing. I could tell my feet were beginning to get beat up. The water bladder in my pack was near empty and the two bottles of Skratch in the front were clogged and impossible for me to drink. I was hot; the sun danced up into the sky and without any cloud or rain reprieve, us ultra runners marching on beneath her.

As I got to the bottom of the road, about to make the turn up into the trees that would spit me into the tiny town of Twin Lakes, Trapper appeared. A hug smile hung above his recognizable purple shirt and playfully strong running stride. I teared up immediately when I noticed him.

"There you are champ!" he called out to me in my elation. "Just up and over this hill, we're all waiting for you on the other side!"

This hill happens to be a short steep climb into an even steeper drop into the Twin Lakes aid station. The last several miles, running above the area, I could see cars and tiny humans preparing for all us runners. I knew this moment was arriving but nothing could prepare me for the outpouring of love I was about to receive.

Dropping down the craggy hill, poles in hand and taking tender, careful steps, I didn't dare yet look up. But a huge smile was already making its way across my face and my body began to experience a new lightness. I heard my name. I looked up and out toward the blow up arches of the aid station and into the roar of joyful humanity. And there were my people: Hallie, who had flown in from Minnesota for a mere twenty four hours just to watch me at this aid station, and Cindi, who had dedicated her Leadville experience to crewing me after she pulled her name out of the race due to an injury.

Cindi held a piece of paper with my name on it. As we jogged through the town toward the tent my crew set up, I was met with cheers and shouts. Don, my ultra running buddy from Fairplay, showed up in a bright Hawaiian button down and as he fell into stride beside me, exclaimed, "You're doing amazing!"

Twin Lakes aid station. I was inside of the experience after witnessing it the year before. Support in the form of rally cries and cheerful shouts, colorful flags and camping chairs of every shape and shade for the bottoms of humans there for each runner passing through. It is the place I want to go to inside of myself when I want to remind my body: this is joy. You are worthy. It's all been here, waiting for you.

And there is Little Barbara, laughing and laughing, rowdy and wild, shirt off and running through the yard with her siblings, with all the freedom and autonomy in the universe.

This is how healing can happen. In those incredible and real moments of our adulthood, we invite our younger selves to come along to play, with all the unconditional love we can offer. And when we can do that, I think we can heal those wounded younger parts of ourselves.

When it was time, I got up from the camping chair.

I strapped on my hydration vest and with fresh socks on my blistered feet, I grabbed my trekking poles and looked up and out toward Hope Pass, the ascent and descent that would take me to the 50-mile turnaround. One of the most challenging sections was upon me. Up to 12,000 feet and over to the halfway point turnaround at Winfield. Then back up and over, once again, to this very place.

There were five smiling, proud faces all beaming my way, mightier than any sun beam on that mountain running day. They were sending me on my way, knowingly hopeful that I would crest the pass and return to them, ready to take on the night miles with Trapper.

"Do your thing! Crush it," Don called out and I raised my poles high into the air with one hand and trotted off with an avocado wrap ready to go in the other. I had done this section as a training run twice over the summer, so I thought I knew what to expect. But, as I would learn, Hope Pass can be anything but predictable.

Once I left the cheer and support of Twin Lakes at Mile 38, it was time for the Creek Crossing and then up to the top of Hope Pass. Cindi had slapped an avocado and mayo wrap in my hand, my request at the day's start for that moment. As my power walk turned into a run, I attempted to nibble the food. My mouth and mind and body all hated that idea. Instead of shoving the calories in, I dropped the wrap to the ground. I remember thinking I was going to regret that. (Spoiler: I did.)

Arriving at the creek crossing, my hands gripped onto the rope as icy water lapped at my calves. With wet shoes, it was time to trudge up a mountain. Poles in hand and hope in my belly, I climbed. The sun sweltered with no reprieve from the heat. As I moved closer to the sun, my legs quivered, and I realized that the heat and rising altitude was getting to me. I focused on increasing my electrolyte consumption and eating what I could from my pack.

This trek to what is called Hopelessness Aid Station at the top of the Pass was, in my mind, one I could tackle. I had done double Hope Pass training runs this summer so I felt ready for all twenty plus miles. But the distance already under my legs mixed with the lack of calories in me meant it was slow going. Very slow, molasses kind of going. I didn't have to go fast. I just had to go.

I remembered for a moment the llamas. In order to get the aid station set up ahead of the runners, volunteers lug up all the necessary supplies using the foot power of these animals. I smiled for a moment as I leaned against my poles, taking a quick breather as my legs quaked from the climb.

Llamas. I get to see llamas.

Around another bend, I came across a runner flopped on the ground, his back pressed against a log, face pale. I stopped, asking him if he was okay.

"Yeah, yeah, I'm good."

I asked if he was drinking water. When I learned he was

cramping up, I pulled out a couple salt tabs from my pack and said, "Take these."

He looked at my palm for a few seconds, not bothering to reach out for my extended gift. A beat passed, no one saying anything.

"Take one," I urged, "It might help."

"Yeah. Thanks." He took them from my outstretched hand, "I'm good, really."

I've been there, I thought. Just in need of a damn breather. I understood. Satisfied that he was going to be okay, I continued.

Mere minutes later, without warning, The Urge struck. Runners know exactly what I mean here.

I had to poop.

And it had to happen right now.

A soft whine escaped my lips as my eyes darted behind me first and then off into the woods. I had to find a spot and it needed to happen as soon as humanly possible.

Fortunately, I was ready for this moment. When I first arrived in Colorado, I had been out on a long training run on a road, an out and back situation. On the way back, The Urge struck and struck hard. In my pack, along with my water, salt tabs, gels, and cell phone, was a little plastic baggie. That baggie was my poo bag: it held toilet paper, single packed wet wipes, and an extra plastic bag. I found that this was a must have in my pack at all times. That run was the first time this mostly-city runner had to use a poo bag for The Urge.

Meanwhile, at 11,500 feet in the sky, I pulled over behind a nearby tree several feet off the trail. It was the only passable place within reason I could squat comfortably. I found a stick and dug a quick hole, got my poo bag ready. As soon as I began to relieve myself, the very runner I helped moments ago came trekking up the trail. I was mid-release. We locked eyes. Whatever he might have felt during our exchange before was no match for this. I burned red, my eyes flying away from his. He scuttled away quickly without uttering a word (thank God) and somehow found the energy to quicken his pace even more up the inclined path.

"Oh well," I murmured to myself. "Gotta do what a girl's gotta do."

I did my thing and scraped loose dirt to bury my handiwork. I picked up my poles, looked up at the treetops, and laughed at the absurdity. We can become such animals in ultra running, returning to our most basic form of nature. I don't have a whole lot of experience with that as many of my ultra running friends do. I loved it. I felt a million times better than when I first pulled off the trail and had renewed energy to take on the last half mile or so, "Let's go, B!" I whispered into the alpine breeze.

I arrived at Hopelessness with a mighty thirst for Coca Cola. The entire climb, red cans had consumed much of my thoughts: sweet, black, cold soda. Dopamine released with every thought of it. I was shaking with desire to get my drug. I slumped into one of the empty chairs at Hopeless Aid Station and a volunteer swooped over.

"What do you need? We have mashed potatoes and water and watermelon..."

I interrupted him, "Coke," I gasped, "Just Coke."

He scrunched his nose, "No Coke up here, love. Can I get you some Gatorade? Mashed potatoes?"

I wanted to cry. My mind had created a glorious story that once I got to Hopelessness, once I was surrounded by the llamas, I could drink the magical elixir.

"Potatoes, please," I managed to squeak.

He nodded kindly and headed toward the tent. "And something cold," I added with a pitiful gasp.

Believe it or not, a person can feel dejected at the top of a mountain on a beautiful day surrounded by happy people, a fire crackling, and llamas munching grass nearby.

Leaving this aid station, the runner is not done climbing. One can see the summit but there is a whole section of switchbacks to navigate upwards before arriving. The prayer poles beckoned up there, the flags whipping in the wind, taunting me of the push I had no choice but to make.

But then, finally, I crested Hope Pass.

A whoosh of air gathered in my lungs and everything quieted. The wind whipped, the flags danced, and the high mountain sun cast its steady light across the whole valley below. My breath caught. I turned around to look back at the winding trail and could see the aid station, the llamas chewing and runners slumped in chairs. And beyond that, Twin Lakes.

I was standing in the sky.

Gratitude surged through me. For my legs, for my people, for the way life opens when we surrender to it. For the thousands of steps and stories that had brought me here. And for the briefest of moments, I felt a hand on my shoulder. Someone was here with me. Ben? Another runner? Didn't matter. I wasn't alone. I was doing it. And I was here.

And just as swiftly, then another thought followed: I have no idea how I'm going to turn around at fifty miles and do this all again.

But, I didn't have to know, I reminded myself. All I had to do was just move. Move forward and keep my body in motion. It was useless to feel sorry for myself.

I Velcro-ed onto my favorite mantra: "Little by little — a little becomes a lot." The steepest part of the mountain was just ahead of me. I had to trek down it as best I could knowing that I must go up it again. And soon. "Little by little, a little becomes a lot," I repeated to myself.

That meant nutrition - bites. Hydration— sips. Movement —steps. Mindset — thoughts.

It is one thing to reach the summit of Hope Pass the first time. It is a whole other thing to power down it to the fifty mile turnaround, then deliberately turn to charge back up and over it again. It was the task at hand. A few runners passed me. I passed a few more. Exchanging few words, we encouraged each other. We were doing the thing. We were on our way.

"Let's just keep going," someone said while laughing as we fell into step together. "It's what we came here for, ain't it?"

Yes it is, I thought. *Shit and all.*

31

Letting Go

I've taken on
the form of
a mighty boulder,
once safe
in a fortitude stillness
atop a sturdy ridge.
But, the just-enough
has bumped me,
the past placed her hands
on my backside
and pushed me
toward future.
I begin my
roll and tumble
into the canyon,
gravity and momentum
my companions.
Don't try to reroute me.
Don't try to stop me.

You'll only
get in my way.

32

Women Endure

Late July before Race Day

It was a bright summer morning in the thick of training, and I'd woken up early. My legs had work to do.

The Colorado Trail snaked off into the trees toward Kenosha Pass. I sat askew in the front seat of my Subaru, door open, legs dangling out the side. Pulling on a fresh sock, I tilted my face to the rising sun and lifted my lips into a smile. A self-supported trail marathon lay ahead of me. My hydration pack was filled to the brim with everything I could need: gels, a baggie with toilet paper, mace spray, salt tabs, headphones and phone, and enough bars to hold me over. I reached into the backseat and rummaged for my dusty trail shoes.

There was a buzz in my chest—the thrill before setting out for big miles. I was easing out of peak training and had one more long push before my taper. Soon, I'd enter two weeks of low mileage, stretching, deep sleep, hydration, and all the carbs I could muster. But not yet; I had this long run ahead of me.

And just then, a truth ran through my blood like lightning: Women endure.

It's one of those realities I've been subtly aware of my whole life. The way my mother folded endless piles of laundry so her kids could tumble in them, streak them with grass stains and gravel dust. The way she rose before sunrise to pray, then balanced babies on her hips and teenagers at the coffee pot. The way she washed a million dishes and put hot meals on the table. The way she woke in the night to crying children and soothed them back to sleep.

Endurance. I saw it in my oldest sister, too—how, as a teen, she also tended to us babies. She held us when we spit up, watched over us with motherly hands. She went on to run the Boston Marathon and, years later, faced a breast cancer diagnosis while continuing to mother her children, to work, to live.

Women endure. I learned it first from them.

Tugging my shoes on, I double-knotted the laces and smoothed sunscreen across my face, shoulders, and neck. The mountain sun was unrelenting, no matter the day's temperature. My skin was precious, and I preferred not to get a burn alongside the usual trials of trail running.

I stooped, stood, twisted my pack onto my shoulders, clasped it around my chest. The familiar weight felt solid, a worthy companion for the trek ahead. I gave my leopard-print shorts a tug from my crotch—comfort gained by an inch.

And then, I was off.

The trail swept up the pass in long, back-and-forth curves. Hikers, dogs, and runners passed me on their way down, grins and friendly hellos exchanged, as is the way of the trail. Ease rushed through me, loosening a grip I hadn't realized I was holding—a body always slightly on guard.

No bears today, I thought with a grin. *Only humans.*

The further up I went, the fewer people I encountered. Soon, I was alone for miles. With one headphone in and one ear out, I stayed alert but relaxed. My body was responding well. At 10,000 feet, I glanced at my watch—steady breath, fluid motion, regular fueling. It was a perfect long-run execution.

At mile 13.1, my turnaround point, I paused. A fallen tree jutted over a drop-off, exposing a brilliant sky and swaying trees. I propped my phone against a log, set a self-timer, and power-posed.

Isn't this all a miracle? I marveled as I flicked through the photos.

And then, surprise. A patch. A splay of red-brown on my white leopard shorts.

I had gotten my period somewhere on the trail.

Embarrassment flushed through me. I thought of all the hikers I'd passed. The hellos. The men, the families, the dogs.

The memory surfaced. As a young adult, I was back in Massachusetts for the holidays with a boyfriend visiting family. I had just gotten my period on the plane ride over, so we stopped at a CVS for tampons and Tylenol. At dinner, he offered aloud to go to the car to get my bag.

"He's going to touch those?" another sister's boyfriend stage-whispered to her, horrified.

I was used to hiding proof of my period.

I got it fir the first time in my late teens on a Sunday morning before church, wearing brand-new white pants. I didn't know how to use a tampon. I found one in my sister's drawer and shoved the entire thing in, plastic applicator and all. At mass, I stood, sat, kneeled, and prayed, sinfully uncomfortable.

By the first reading, blood was visibly spotting between my legs. I tied a jacket around my waist, squeezed my thighs together, and penguin-walked to the bathroom. I tore out the plastic applicator as the priest murmured, "This is the blood of Christ."

How do women do this?

We just do. Quietly. Shamefully. Invisibly.

And yet, we endure.

I looked again at my photos—my posture, my expression. Triumphant. Arms crossed, one leg up. A fierce smile.

So why the shame? Why had I automatically wanted to hide? I had just run 13 miles and was about to run 13 more. There was no one to explain or justify to, no reason to make myself small.

Why hide at all?

My chest lifted with the unlearning.

I would not hide this. I would run—bloody and bold and proud.

Pressing start on my watch, I turned back down the trail.

I am a woman, I thought. *I endure.*

It became my mantra. I passed more hikers—kids, dogs, couples—and I didn't shrink or cover up. I just ran. Head up. Chest out. Taylor Swift in my ears.

I exited the trail with dried salt on my cheeks, dirt streaks down my legs, and a browning blood splotch between my thighs.

And that night, I posted the photo with the notation that I am a woman. And I endure. Blood and all.

Why should I be ashamed? Why should I hide proof of my existence? My body's capability to create life?

The response to my photo delighted me. Friends — both

men and women — commented with enthusiasm and support. Someone even said, "This deserves to go viral." No shame. No shrinking. Just love. Empowerment. A shared celebration of strength. It felt like the right punctuation to a full, rich day.

Who is afraid of this?

After a hot shower, I inserted a tampon the right way. And I fell asleep with a small, satisfied smile on my face.

I am a woman. And women endure.

33

The Rattle at My Shoulder

Early August before Race Day

A few weeks before race day, my mother sent me a small medal of Mother Teresa — the Catholic nun and saint revered for her service to the poor and dying in Calcutta, India.

The medal had a lineage.

Years earlier, a client of mine — a woman in her early seventies with wisps of silver hair and a face carved by decades of stories — had pressed it into my hands after a coaching session. She had received it while on a spiritual trip to India, where she visited the Missionaries of Charity and received the medal, already blessed, from a nun there.

"Your mom should have Mother Teresa's love," she had said, folding the envelope into my palm with gentle conviction.

So, from Mother Teresa, to my client, to my hands — and

then to my mother's. I mailed it that same afternoon from Minnesota to Western Massachusetts.

Years passed.

And then, in Colorado, the envelope reappeared. My name written in her familiar script.

When I opened it, the small metal oval tumbled into my hand. The imprint of Mother Teresa's face caught the light. I pressed my thumb over the surface and felt a lump rise in my throat.

From one mother to another, and now, to me.

She sent it with no note, only the quiet understanding that I would know what it meant. I did.

My mother — devout, traditional, unwavering in her Catholic faith — had once held this token as her own. She knew I had stepped away from the Church. She knew I did not share her religious convictions. Still, she sent it. Not because she expected me to believe what she believed, but because she loved me. And this, for her, was love made tangible.

I didn't plan to bring anything "sacred" with me to Leadville, but this felt right. Not because I believed it would protect me from blisters or altitude or the dark unknowns of the trail — but because I wanted to carry love, too. I wanted to remember that I'm not alone.

I pinned it to the free loop on the left shoulder strap of my hydration pack.

It rattled gently — like a whisper, like a prayer — through every mile of the Leadville 100.

In the mountain silence, in the dust, through blisters and creek crossings, with nausea curling through my gut and peace finding home within me — it was there. Swinging lightly with each step. The quiet blessing of women who fiercely believed in their own way.

Even though I couldn't hold Catholicism as my faith, and the medal had no literal religious significance to me, I could run with the love it represented. I could run with the strength passed down through hands that knew labor, prayer, heartbreak, and endurance. From one enduring woman to another.

I thought back to when my mother asked me to say "I love you, I'm sorry" to the bees in the side yard. That strange, tender moment of repair — a mix of mysticism and maternal instinct. She believed in healing through reverence. And, in some quiet way, I did too.

That small token, gifted and re-gifted over decades and continents, carried what mattered most: the intention to protect, to bless and honor our chosen path in life. The chain of care between women, between mothers and daughters, between seekers and the sacred. A connection between women who endure.

It did not need to mean everything to me. But it meant enough, rattling there at my shoulder.

> *"Life is an opportunity, benefit from it.*
> *Life is beauty, admire it.*
> *Life is a dream, realize it.*
> *Life is a challenge, meet it.*
> *Life is a duty, complete it.*
> *Life is a game, play it.*
> *Life is a promise, fulfill it.*
> *Life is sorrow, overcome it.*
> *Life is a song, sing it.*
> *Life is a struggle, accept it.*
> *Life is a tragedy, confront it.*
> *Life is an adventure, dare it.*
> *Life is luck, make it.*
> *Life is too precious, do not destroy it.*
> *Life is life, fight for it."*
> *— Mother Teresa*

34

Mountain Woman

Today I met
a mountain woman.
She told me
about the sickness
she gets
coming down
the mountain,
not up.
I understood that
as grief—
why must we
depart
from our
highest self?

35

"Nuanced" is My Favorite Word

The Leadville 100: Arriving at Twin Lakes Inbound, 62 miles

When I returned to Twin Lakes I was overwhelmingly relieved
– My people! Clean clothes! Fresh shoes! My pacer!

The sun had dropped and my headlamp was now slicing
through the darkening air. The creek crossing on the way
back brought with it an army of mosquito bites and I was eager
for a reset at the aid station. The final miles from the base of
Hope Pass felt demoralizing. My feet ached as though I'd been
barefoot on rocks all day. My body needed food, but my mouth
was so dry. The sun left for the day, no longer a comfort to my
eyesight and skin, and I wouldn't have her company for a long
time. The darkness had fallen. I was getting cold.

That relief soon turned to slight despair. There were many
more miles to go. A whole night stretched ahead of me, a
mighty yawn of forever. I crumpled into the folding camper
chair and promptly burst into tears. It had taken me longer

than I anticipated to drop back down the front side of Hope, walking down the inclines when all I wanted to do was run them. My body was in full protest.

"I'm not an athlete!" I cried. I couldn't see myself clearly.

Cindi rolled her eyes lovingly at me and Chris kissed me softly on the cheek, rubbing my shoulders as he did so. Hallie laughed and told me, "You are a god damn athlete!"

Someone shimmied my wet shoes off my feet and pulled dry socks on the left then right. Arms wrapped around me as my crew fell into action. Someone else chuckled lightly, a kindness to the sound, reminding me that I just ran 60 plus miles at 10,000 feet altitude and climbed up and over a mountain – twice. My shoes came off as I sat obediently and I replace my wet sports bra as someone massaged my calves and feet.

"Here, eat what looks good to you," Cindi prompted me.

I gave in and picked up a fig bar.

Beliefs can move us or derail us. They narrate our days with a flair—sometimes poetic, sometimes punishing. They'd clouded so much of my life, these thoughts, these inherited stories. Many times, the conditions of our realities can be enough to push us over the edge when we have a tired mind.

There were pizza slices in the tent, and I attempted to chew the bread and cheese, willing my throat to do its job and swallow the damn thing. It was tortuous. A cookie appeared and I nibbled at it. Somehow, cold grapes made their way into my pack.

A decision was made by the group: I'd go into the night with gels and grapes in my vest, electrolyte-laden water in my hydro pack, but no extra bottles of Skratch liquid fuel. Up until then, it was the bulk of my calories. I managed mashed potatoes and watermelon, sure. But those bottles had me moving through the most challenging climbs. Looking back, I wish I had the head space and wherewithal to challenge that idea. It was not the right call. Late into the race, I'd struggle to eat and would have benefited greatly from liquid nutrition.

I'm learning that happens in races — and in life. The roads are paved with good intentions, for most of us. There was good intent behind that decision – I'd lighten up, probably get a boost of positive energy from slightly less pressure on my mangled feet. It could have been the right call in any other circumstance. My crew was looking out for me. But when a runner doesn't get the energy source they need to move in the first place, none of that lack of weight matters.

As a result of that one decision, I ate even less and suffered even more. But, there's no escaping the pain. It's bound to happen, arriving in some shape. If not this, then that or something else. That's okay; that's part of the ultra running game. And more so, that's part of life. Life circumstances unfold and they simply lead us somewhere new.

My mind wandered as I loped through the trails with Trapper, remembering the one morning, midsummer at the cabin, when the water stopped flowing.

I was returning from a sunrise walk. A German Shepherd at the end of our road had shot out of his yard and nipped my arm. He didn't break any skin, but I had to use my stern, commanding voice to usher him away. No owner nearby.

My heart knocked at my ribs as I opened the cabin door. Hankering for a good shower, I turned the spigot. Creaks and squeaks, but no rushing water. Only a few droplets released.

The well had some sort of clog and my roommate Tucker was on the case. Jostling with the levers in the basement, he managed to restore the water after this first incident. Then, again when it happened a second time. By the third time around, there was nothing he could do to get the pipes flowing and we found ourselves dry as dry could be on the Fourth of July.

There was only one "well guy" in the area and graciously he arrived on the holiday with his crew to tend to our problem. And when he fully fixed it, I'm sure the hikers over on Hoosier's Pass could hear us whooping and cheering.

During those few water-less days, I learned that it took several gallons just to flush a toilet. Buying water from the gas station twenty minutes away was expensive and laborious. Thankfully, nature gives up copious amounts of water that time of year. The snow was melting, and the fresh cold water ran down the mountain into reservoirs and lakes. We had access to tons of it. Back and forth from across the rocky lane from the cabin to a small waterfall, I collected as much as I could. The dining room table was a collection of receptacles that my roommate and I took to filling in our down time. Every time we needed to flush, at least two of those gallons went into the tank.

Another morning, a sinkhole appeared on the dirt road, about a hundred meters from our home. The gush of water across the road corroded the structure of it and in no time a hole three quarters of the road's length appeared. Deep enough to wreak havoc on any car trying to drive over it. We parked our cars further down the mountain and walked the short way toward our home. Which meant if we arrived home after dark, we had to be wary of the neighborhood bears.

Bears don't want to hurt you, I'd remind myself as I cut my car engine and prepared to jog up to my front door. The millions of stars above and their leader the moon provided partial light; I clicked on a flashlight, started singing aloud, and scurried home.

Good practice for Leadville! I remembered noting.

Calls to the town might as well have been notes in a bottle down the waterfalls. It took many days, then weeks, for anyone to size up the hole (visit 1), place orange cones around it (visit 2), and then finally fill it up for our safety.

Soon we could pull our cars right up to the cabin again. I didn't have to be on guard. I didn't have to retrieve water for the toilets. I had a hot shower and a warm bed and this beautiful experience in Alma, Colorado to call my own.

What else have I taken for granted? What other parts of my life were filled with nuance?

It was a question that I couldn't help but ask. So much in my life felt nuanced, textured, neither good nor bad, not black or white.

I thought of my partner, Chris, and the way he held me, like a lake where I could be buoyant and free. I thought of the space he gave me to be my own person, to float or to swim or to hold onto him for safety as needed. I remembered how I cried in his arms in the painful retelling of my sexual assault. How he listened, how he kissed my face, how he told me he loved me, how it wasn't my fault. I felt safe there with him.

I thought of my mother, the giver, the creator of life and the fierce believer in her God, her religion. I thought of her power, the way she met her life with a ferocity that only now, with distance, could I see as admirable. She wanted a spiritual life for her children, Catholicism her path toward redemption and transcendence. And I took my own way, still discovering it as I charter unknown territories.

I thought of my God, of how I believed her to be, of the stories told to me about my place in the Universe over the years, and all the unlearning I committed to do. Of how Colorado that summer felt like home and vacation and work and worship.

I thought of my brother in Puerto Rico and how I wanted to protect him from what happened to me. I thought of my boyfriend in college and how he couldn't know the whole story (until now — he helped edit this book). I thought of the bees and my brother Joe, the ways I felt so scared and yet so taken care of, simultaneously. Of my father's response to red rage — and his own red rage.

I thought more of my father, his steadiness to his wife and their shared God. His vision of a big family and a doting wife and obedient kids. How his hands worked the earth and planted and tended the gardens. The same hands that spanked children and governed inmates, wore a wedding ring and held the Bible, threw plates and shoved my brothers, pointed to the stars and held my hand on nature walks. I thought of his complexity. He wanted a life of goodness for his family, to be seen as moral and righteous; and he did it all imperfectly in the ways he knew how.

Perhaps we need to plunge into a darkness before we can fully see the light and the love for what it is. Perhaps we need a clogged well and a sinkhole to get thinking in a more complex way about life. Perhaps we need a bit of space and time to give each other the grace we deserve.

As my pacer, Trapper, and I headed out into the night, another memory overtook me and I buckled momentarily. The image was vibrant and something inside me clicked into place. Confidence washed over me in mere seconds, my chest swelled with renewed certainty – I was going to finish this this thing.

Once again, I knew. And it was my teenage self, reminding me.

I was a senior in high school and one of the co-captains of my cross country team. We were nearing the end of our season and had performed well. The day of our greatest race had arrived. We were to compete on our home course against our biggest rival. They were unbeatable. We were hungry and ready for a race.

Coach Goda, also the geometry and physics teacher, called the co-captains into his homeroom late that morning. It was raining sideways, with temps in the very cool and uncomfortable high 30's/low 40's. Puddles had begun to form. The weather was bound to hold.

"We have every right to call a rain delay and move the race to another day," Coach said, arms crossed against his crumpled button down. "What do you both want to do?"

It was my earliest memory of an adult handing over decision power to me. I was seventeen and I wanted to run. Running was the very thing I woke for, went to school for, ate for, lived for.

Running gave me moments like this, moments I did not have in my patriarchal, Catholic home. Moments where I felt empowered, given decision power. I was ready. I knew the girls on my team were ready. And I was not going to let mere weather change the tides for us.

"We're running," I had said. "We're running and we're going to win."

There's a photo from that day. Its image flickered as I gathered up my poles in real time and began trekking up mini-Mt Elbert in Leadville, Trapper chattering beside me.

In that photo, my high school team gathered together at the gated entrance to the puddled reservoir. I have a towel wrapped around my shoulders. The team is gathered close and smiling at the camera, hoods pulled over tangled wet hair and mud splashes on tired legs.

We'd won the meet by a single point.

It wasn't pretty and there was enough suffering involved over the 2.7-mile course. We fought, we pushed, we moved with purpose. We knew we had a fighting chance to win– but only if we showed up, gave it all we had, and left our legs out there on the course.

We won. But barely. Only a point. But, with everything we had. If one runner had a different day that afternoon, it'd be different.

My headlamp jostled, offering me enough light to see the next step I needed to take. Spiders dashed across the trail and I kicked a few loose rocks as I shuffled uphill. I was hurting.

But – I was in fresh clothes and I was warm. I was with a friend. I had shown up. I was choosing, every minute, to move forward. And I was ready to see what might happen if I just kept putting a foot in front of the other.

There was so much behind me; there was so much ahead.

Suffering and pain and bliss and glory. Good stories and their beliefs, good intentions and their realities. It's all here, all part of life, all part of this race. Texture. Complexity.

We moved together through the shadows, legs tired but steady. I held the past in one hand, the future in the other.

Nuanced, I thought as we moved in the moonlight. *Nuanced is my favorite word.*

36

Common Ground

Mere days before Race Day

The Tuesday before race day, my dad visited me for two nights in Colorado.

When I was a child, we'd have our day adventures: an afternoon at Home Depot, a fishing trip on a canoe, a hike on the 7 Sisters Trail. Over the years into my early adulthood, he had a way of showing up for the big things: moving me into my college dorm and getting me situated in New York City when I got a job with Nike.

Yet one day, like the cabin's water spigot, access to my dad turned off. Between college and adulthood, I faded off into a life of my own. I blossomed into my own person, unfurling into all the roles of who I was outside of daughter and sister. I was a runner, a coach, a partner, and an auntie. I was a mentor, a colleague, and a pet parent. The role of father's daughter sputtered and stalled out, undernourished. We hugged at

Christmas when I visited. Every so often, he answered the phone before my mom could when I called to check in. Space naturally formed between us, a cavity, a lifetime of words left unsaid. I held my hurts and hopes to myself, my innermost world held in bubble wrap and securely locked away. I still felt small in his presence.

So, when he said he was going to fly into Denver, rent a car, book a hotel nearby in Fairplay, all the week before my big race — I was at first taken aback. I wanted to keep my pre-race week light, bright, and without complication. I almost said no. Instead, I looked to the trees for answers, tossing questions to the birds like seeds. The mourning dove and the dark-eyed junco, chickadee and robin, all seemed to offer one thing: allow.

Allow as an opportunity to try something hard and see what I was made of in the process. Allow as an opportunity to heal something in our relationship. Simply allow.

And allow I did.

I took my dad out to my favorite town near Leadville, Buena Vista. The town center was a few blocks of old western road lined with antique shops, restaurants, outdoor goods shops, and mountain wear boutiques. The sun blazed between momentary downpours of temperamental stormy weather. I booked us an afternoon adventure at a hot spring, complete with a cold plunge area in a mountain stream. We met a few other runners there who were racing that weekend, and I listened to my dad crow about his beautiful daughter who was going to race it, too.

"I'll be cheering her on!"

I wrangled in real time with my feelings as I moved from hot soak to the gushing chill of the cold-water plunge. Warmth from his attention, words of affirmation, a sudden show of support. Frozen with a shiver from the silence of everything left unsaid. Hot and cold.

Walking through town, he watched me as I laughed at little kids running through a public sprinkler. With tangled hair, hands splayed upward as their bare feet slapped the wet pavement, their energy was palpable. They were the essence of what I wanted to feel during my race: all play and presence and delight.

I turned to tell my dad this, to pop a champagne truth, when he interrupted, "You'd make such a great mom."

A mother or a nun, I remembered.

I swallowed my insights, and the bubble wrap tightened, somehow re-corking the feeling. We got into the rental car, and I said plainly with a shrug, "I decided to do something else with my life." I was back up in the tree house, alone, waiting for Dad to notice I was missing from the moment. Instead, he turned the car key. I looked out the window. And the moment passed us by.

We drove toward the nearby hiking trails in silence watching the storm roll past, the clouds a charcoal smudge across the sky. Rain fell. Then stopped. Then fell again. Unpredictable bouts.

When we parked at the trail head the storm had blown in another direction and a bluebird sky canopied us. A gravel road forked ahead: to the right were craggy slopes and to the left was a sparkling lake full of reflection. I inhaled the scenery. I imagined my younger self with us, tangled hair and barefoot. I imagined taking her hand in my heart and gave it a squeeze of affection. Together, we walked into the forest with my dad.

Then we all did what we did best together: we marveled.

This. This is holy.

Across the lake a bride gripped onto her groom, a photographer capturing their moment. A yellow warbler sang from the aspens. Mossy rocks emerged from the water's edge and ripples nearby gave away the location of a rainbow trout.

Our kind of holy, I reminded the little girl I had brought with us. Wide-eyed and delighted, she ran off the trail to explore the remnants of a ghost mill still standing in the wood. Dad watched without a word, but I felt his reverence.

As we walked together up an incline toward an alpine waterfall, he began to talk. Bit by bit, he shared about his own father. How his dad hit him when his collar was crooked, an undeserving punishment for a normal kid thing. I'm not sure why he started telling me his stories. Perhaps it was his way of honoring the moment or recognizing the importance of connection through storytelling — another thing we shared deeply. I can barely count on one hand the number of times my dad was vulnerable and real with me. But here he was, now, in his own way, sharing his own little kid truths.

My dad told me he wasn't loved in the way he needed — not so much those words, but in sentiment. For the first time, I could see him as a little boy who grew into an adult. An adult who claimed his identity and values through a religion. Who had a strong idea of what good values looked like and imposed that upon his children the ways he knew how.

Not so unlike me, I thought. I'd become an adult who claimed my identity and values from my community of runners and other like-minded souls.

"See me," he seemed to say. "Respect me. Love me."

The little girl in me murmured it back, "See me. Respect me. Love me."

We hiked the short path along the trees, the perfect mountain lake to one side. Hands on hips, we moved in adoration of the sun, her heat on our exposed faces. We watched as a mama goat and her kid wandered nearby, allowing us to come close. Marveling together, we soaked in one of the only dialects that we shared: appreciation of Mother Nature and all the possibilities within Her kingdom.

We speak two languages, both a request for respect in different dialects. But, as I listened to his language, the way his tongue formed words, phrases, and well-recited tunes, I realized that maybe I CAN forgive. Maybe I can release my hold on blame and expectation. Maybe we can heal.

We set back toward his hotel in Fairplay where my car was parked, readying to say goodbye. I was eager to slip into my pre-race mindset. The start line was two sleeps away. We watched the mountains pass us by and I asked him what he wanted to listen to.

"John Denver!" He exclaimed. Specifically Take Me Home Country Roads, about the state of West Virginia where my father spent many a day in his young life. He sang, looking over at me with the eyes he gave me, prompting me to join him. I shyly joined, the whole endeavor feeling more intimate than I knew what to do with.

A memory flashed back. I was a teenager in the passenger seat with my father as we drove toward some errand I didn't want to be on. He reached over and turned down Rush Limbaugh on the radio, blessing us with a silent vehicle. In the hush of a truck rattling down the road, he then asked me: "Am I a good father?" I froze. I was fourteen, maybe fifteen. I had felt largely overlooked and grandly judged by this man. I was supposed to be going to a church of his choosing to learn rules that didn't serve me as a young woman. I felt pinned, unsure what to say back, unsure what prompted the question. It was the most real I remember my dad ever being with me. In my freeze state, I said something like, "Yeah, sure."

Once we arrived at the hotel. I lingered for a few moments, eating cheese and crackers as he sipped red wine. We called a few of my siblings, their faces filling up the phone screen with wide smiles as they answered. It created enough space between me and dad – there was no more room for truth, no more space for one-on-one connection, when wine and phone calls were in the room. No room for him to ask me again, "Am I good father?"

This is okay, I thought. *This is all we have. This is my father. I am his daughter.*

We hugged at the doorway as I said, "Thanks for coming, Dad." And I meant it.

I stepped out into the parking lot at the motel and looked up. The sky was streaked with pink and purple smears, a celebration of ... something. I patted my heart. "I love you Barbara," I whispered, thankful my inner child joined us for the day. I wondered what teenage me would have responded back in that truck ride to my father.

As I got into my car and closed the door, Dad suddenly came hustling out the side door.

In hand he had a small plastic bottle, a tiny cross scrawled in black sharpie on it. I rolled the window down, Taylor Swift softly playing from the dusty speakers.

"You haven't gotten your blessing," he said.

We all say "I love you" in our own way. And like Ben, my dad rolls with Jesus.

He had his serious church face on, the one I remembered well from childhood. Dad was regularly involved every Sunday;

most often it was up in the choir, singing proudly through the crackling mic. Otherwise, he was alongside the priest handing out the holy wafers or sips of wine at Communion. Wherever he stood, he had a downcast, pious face, as though Michelangelo carved my father right then and there as a devout disciple. It was jarring to me as a child. I'd watch him, perplexed, knowing that this face could contort with red emotion. As an adult, I now know he was speaking to his God. I now could see the complexity of sides of him: Warm and then cold; storming and then clear skies. Nuanced.

This is how he says I love you, I inhaled the reminder.

I thought back to how he took interest in the race and the enormity of this moment in my life. How we enjoyed the landscape of Colorado together. I had shown him my cabin and the little town I inhabited. And at one point, I drove him to the base of Hope Pass, pointing to the clearing between mountain ridges and said, "I'll be climbing up and over that this weekend." I wanted him to be proud of me, as all children do. And I realized, I wanted him to feel like he was a good father.

He pressed his thumb to the bottle before transporting it to the top of my head. I didn't close my eyes or look down. Instead, I watched him. He shut his eyes, bowed his head and traced a cross on my forehead. Murmuring a blessing for my safety and success in the race, he called upon Jesus. I felt my little girl self retreating to a dark corner inside of me, but I remained still, allowing him to continue.

"Thanks, Dad," I gave a half wave and a tight-lipped smile as he walked back to his hotel room.

Then, without really thinking, I swept my hand up to my skin and wiped the moisture away.

My body didn't want to comply. I didn't want to give an inch of my body away anymore, even to acquiesce to how my dad loves. I wanted my little girl self to feel seen and tended to, instead. He was showing love as he could. And I was showing love, as I could.

"Disrespectful," I could hear a voice of authority tell me from my right shoulder.

"It's your body," said the grown-up Barbara to the young girl inside of me.

"Thank you," she whispered back.

We don't always get love in the ways we need it when we need it most.

I felt the familiar ache for him to pull me into a genuine hug and tell me how proud he was of me. How strong I was. To look me in the eyes and tell me how incredibly lucky he was to have me as his daughter. To ask me again but in a new way: "What do you need for me to be a good father?"

Instead, I got a blessing from a religion that was never mine. I was his way of saying, "I love you."

This is okay, I thought. *This is all we have. This is my father. I am his daughter.*

I drove away into my quiet life. I turned up the boy band O-Town on the speakers for my younger self. Windows down, the cool air rushed in and my hair tangled as I sang along.

I had a race to run in just two days. And I knew I was going to make such a good ultra runner.

37

How I Love (anything)

I love
in the way
the ocean does:
lapping the shore
in adoration
then retreating
back to one's
sure self,
always to
return
then leave
again
and again.

38

Seeing Things (All the Way Through)

The Leadville 100: Somewhere within 70–80 miles

"Look up!" Trapper crowed.

It was pitch-black and the only light were the beams of white and yellow from our combined headlamps.

I covered my light as I turned my eyes upward. The night was lit with sparkling stars smattering across the chalkboard sky, little-yet-mighty chalk dust lessons left behind many millions or billions of years ago. I immediately felt the same – little-yet-mighty. I was a star, too, comprised of their carbons, their dust, their power. Could they also see me? Will I also keep shining well after my time, moving something mighty in someone else to move forward?

I've never known a world without stars. As a child, I'd lay out on the bed of my dad's truck, wrapped up in a blanket I pulled off some bunk bed inside the farmhouse, and kept watch for shooting stars. Many a summer night, I'd trek out through the back field to a campsite where I'd curl up for warmth with a sister and tilt my face up to the night sky, away from the crackle of the campfire. I'd count as many blazing orbs as I could through the trees, searching for familiar favorites like the Big Dipper and Orion.

Later years, in college, I took an astronomy class at Bentley, the business school in Waltham, Massachusetts. We'd pile up in vehicles and take off far away from the city smog to peer into telescopes and seek out the not-so-familiar constellations. I've forgotten all the names and numbers and data from that college course, but I'll forever remember the feeling of starlit greatness in my bones. My classmates would look through that telescope and seek out the right constellations. I'd look through and lose myself to the swirling delight of brightness conquering even the darkest swallow of space.

"Let's run," my lips moved to speak just as my legs obediently quickened. My mind was its own dark swallow of space. My feet throbbed and I hadn't been able to eat anything substantial for hours. I managed to get some grapes into my belly and a much-too-sugary-for-my-taste sports gel, but it wasn't enough to keep me properly fueled. My body was heavy and tired; my mind was following suit.

And there, step for step, stride for stride with me, was Trapper. The most positive, optimistic, encouraging soul I could ever encounter, let alone have the privilege of his time and energy for my race. In many ultras, runners are given the opportunity to have one or a few pacers. These are runners who can join the racer for stretches of time to keep them going. In Leadville, you are allowed a pacer around mile 62 at Twin Lakes aid station. This pacer can join you for the full 38 miles – which is what Trapper did– or the runner can swap out pacers at each aid station returning home.

Pacers can change everything. They can tell you to look up and look out, changing your perspective on the moment. They can talk to you about nothing and everything, swaying your attention away from the pain in your feet or legs. They can monitor your nutrition, ensuring that you eat when you can and drink before you need to. When in the depths of our own minds, it can mean everything to have another human pull you up and out.

Every time I started running after power walking, he cheered me on.

Never was I swallowed up into mental dark spaces because I had his company. I drew inward a few times, and he encouraged me back out.

We do not heal alone. We do not run ultras alone. Stars do not glimmer alone. We are one of many. A star in a constellation, a constellation in a universe. In it together.

Poles in hand, headlamp forward, breath heaving as steady as I could keep it – I moved ahead with Trapper by my side.

* * *

Something moved in the bushes without making a sound. Trapper was telling a story with fog-breathed words and, half-listening, I snapped my head toward the movement. Shadows swirled then danced away, skittish from my headlamp.

When I was twelve, I got my own bedroom for a few months after construction of an addition was completed on the farmhouse. This was a special privilege; usually, it wasn't until freshman year of high school when older siblings moved up and out of the home to college that a room became available. Until then, I slept with four sisters, two bunk beds, and a crib. For the first time at twelve, I was sleeping alone.

That night terrified me. Without the warmth of my siblings near me, breathing, talking in their sleep, and occasional sleepwalking, I was exposed and vulnerable. A part of me wanted to be a fierce and independent girl, able to sleep in her own room all by herself. I had begged for that room. But once I was there, I was scared to be alone in it.

Once the lights were off, I laid wide-eyed with the blankets curled at my chin. Black shapes would soon ooze across the walls, sliding toward the corners of the room and underneath the shelves on the wall opposite my bed. Grotesque outlines suggested winged creatures with long, muscular legs and horns.

I tried to be brave. I pulled the blankets over my face, I turned over to face the other way, I hummed soft songs, and I prayed to St. Michael the archangel: *Defend me in battle, be my protection against the wickedness and snares of the devil,* I quivered.

Not able to withstand it, I finally began to cry out, "Mama! Ma!"

Mom padded into the room with a hush, her bare feet tiptoeing everywhere she went. Her hands found my forehead, cool, calm, and certain, and began to brush my hair away with gentle strokes.

"There are demons on the wall, Mama," I sniffled.

She reassured me that Jesus would send them away, that he'd make sure I was safe, that everything was okay. Her hands moved from my forehead to my back, rubbing up and down as she began to sing me a church song: *"Be not afraid. I go before you always. Come, follow me. And I will give you rest."*

The words of this song fluttered through me in Colorado as I watched the shadows shape shift into a rock. The beginning lines of the song struck me suddenly, a crescendo of memory lighting up neuron pathways long-still: *You shall cross the barren desert,/but you shall not die of thirst. / You shall wander far in safety/ though you do not know the way.*

I stumbled on a rock, and Trapper shot his arm to catch me.

I almost burst into a sob, instead making a sound like a choked back bit of surprise from the fall. I checked in with myself: there was a canyon carved into my chest and the grief I'd held onto through the years wailed like wind through it. My mother was not able to hold my hand, walk with me to confront my fears, like she did so long ago with the bees.

But, her cooling touch could surface in the middle of the night on a rocky trail, rubbing my back, reassuring me I was brave. *Be not afraid.*

I was in a state of great fatigue and fatigue plays awful games to the mind. I wasn't eating anywhere near enough for calories on the trail. I was twenty hours into nonstop motion (sans the aid station sit downs). My mind, undernourished and flickering like an old TV set, caught sight of new shapes in the woods. Hallucinations. Like the images on the wall as a child.

But this time, the Lorax sat on a rock and Dr Seuss trees draped this way and that. Every now and then, a lobster scuttled across the trail. These were far from demons. These were far from reckless men. These were far from my father's anger and the Church's rules and the sting of the patriarchy. There was not a thing to be frightened of on that trail. There were only a handful of runners with their headlamps jostling along the dirt, the wind whistling through treetops reaching toward the stars. Creatures may be lurking but I could not find any part of me that was scared of them.

I was safe here.

I had my body. My marvelous body and the triumphant mind that came along with it. I had my pack, my running shoes, and warm clothes and Trapper and I had Chris and Cindi and Hallie and Don waiting for me at the finish line.

I was safe here, in my body, on this trail. My mother's cooling touch faded.

211

Trapper pressed power on the speaker attached to his pack and within moments music fed me forward. The Lorax and Dr Suess trees and the lobsters and memories of demons all faded into the black behind us.

* * *

There will forever be something special about watching the sun rise. Then fall. Then rise again. Because, we rise. We fall. We rise again — don't we?

I made it back to Turquoise Lake. In my mind, well ahead of this race, I believed that once I got through the final aid station, it would be mere moments until I arrived at the finish line. That I could pull my way through the final twelve miles and get the damn thing done.

Nothing in my life to date has felt longer than those final miles of Leadville.

I shuffled. I would run for about a minute, then pull back into a walk. The grapes were long gone. The gels had disappeared into my belly and my teeth hurt from the day of ingesting simple sugars. I might have had more in my pockets, but I can't remember if I checked or not. There was one and only one quest: to get to the finish before the thirty-hour cut off mark.

These last miles were a blur of delirium. Nothing looked familiar, even though I had been on those very trails twenty four hours before, as well as a handful of times in my training. The night stretched onward into a pit of forever. I'm sure

Trapper and I talked in those miles. I'm sure he motivated me, supported me, praised me for running again after a three-minute walking spell. My brain did not and could not hold onto the information so that it could remain a retrievable memory.

What I do remember, what my brain held onto, was the slice of purple light rising over the lake that morning. And every spirit that light brought with it.

Beginnings are everywhere. Even in the dark depths of a stretching forever, like this race. Even in the slog of one foot in front of the other. A beginning can, and does, emerge. It all depends on what we choose to see.

My eyes were leaking. I was flooded with flashing images, one after the other, like an old time picture show: Ben, running ahead of me, his smile perceptible even from the back side. *Keep going*, he was saying, checking his heart rate and smiling big. *This is the path, this is the way.*

My father, standing on the edge of the trail, a softness on his face, my mother's hand in his. For a moment I imagined him whispering to me, "I love you, Barbara. I'm sorry."

Did I hear that right? Was that the wind?

I stumbled over a gathering of rocks on the trail and managed to stay upright. Trapper coaxed me forward.

More emerged.

Nieces and nephews crawling atop each other, a pandemonium of toddlers, my siblings gathered as they grasped and held and chased their babies, glancing my way, cheering me on. Proud.

My high school coach with a stopwatch in hand, urging: *Let's go B Powell!* My college coach with his Bentley College cap firmly pulled over his forehead, nodding with his arms folded across his chest. *Champ, keep working.*

The women who knew – who held the secrets of their religions and fathers and lovers and abusers – fists in the air, running in a united pack. I lifted my trekking poles, amazed at the fortitude swirling around me.

And then Chris, his soft eyes and balanced spirit, materialized at my side. He gently pressed his hand to my back, a feather-light kiss on my cheek: *C'mon, honey. You got this.*

I was safe on this trail. I was powerful on this trail. I was broken down and tired as all hell, but I was moving forward. I had too many people at my side to quit now.

My walk quickened to a slow jog and Trapper whooped in support. Perhaps he thought the press of purple morning light was seeping into my legs and giving me my mojo back. I held it all in, holding my pictures with reverence. *My people are here.*

I am becoming brand new, a beginning, all over again.

Taking the next step forward.

That's all I needed to do to make it across the finish line in 28 hours, 15 minutes, and 46 seconds.

39

A Finish Line

The Leadville 100: The Finish Line

"You're about to be a hundred mile finisher!"

Bleary-eyed, I made a point to look up ahead of my aching body. There, in the short-yet-wild distance was the finish line on 6th and Harrison. The place where it all began yesterday. My feet throbbed. My legs were heavy and stiff – but I was still moving. I Had somehow made my way out of the dust of the Boulevard and turned onto the pavement toward the town center.

My vision narrowed. I was aware of people cheering for me from the sidewalks but I couldn't make them out. The only shapes I had eyes for were the looming finish line arches and the people by my side.

Trapper was at my left. I had no idea how he was feeling or what was going on inside of him. Over the night, he never let on. He did the job he came out to do and showered me with positive support the entire way.

Cindi was behind me, phone in hand, telling me I was about to be a finisher. Her tenacity and intense focus on the race, on my success, was evident at every aid station I saw her at. She was the one to get me warm, get me fed when I was able to eat, and make sure I was set up for the next bout of miles before I would see her and the crew again.

And then, there was Chris. Sweet, incredible Chris. He believed in me. Gave me the space I needed this summer. We had our rocky moments. And even throughout uncertainty, he showed up for me. He was at my side when it counted, when it mattered most. Tears sprung to my eyes as I realized that he had always been like that. He didn't just say he was cheering me on. He proved it.

"Let's run!" Trapper's encouragement, right to the very end, lifted my legs off the ground. Together, the four of us began to run our way toward the storied finish line. I heard my name from the crowd, seeing the familiar faces from the Life Time Foundation. I couldn't help but look over at Chris and watch him run at 10,000 feet altitude. He was gasping for breath, eyes focused on the ground, doing what he needed to do to encourage me to complete this unforgettable race. His own way in that moment of delivering a feathery kiss to my cheek, encouraging me on.

And then – I was done.

Just like that, the race was over.

Ken and Merilee, the race founders, were congratulating me and placing a medal around my head. Don was hugging me. Cameras snapped to the tune of a crowded roadside of people. My legs pulsed. My heart slowed. My eyes blurred.

It was over.

A hundred miles. Twenty-eight hours. Hundreds of smiles and thousands of eclectic moments. Hours of aching feet. One sunrise to sunset to another sunrise. The weekends of double long runs and living at altitude and the mountain life I had created all for this moment.

It was over.

I hobbled over to the grass and somehow melted onto it. Someone handed me a beer. Another person handed me a doughnut. After consuming a couple hundred calories over the last ten hours, one would think that I would want to devour those treats. But, instead, I nibbled. I sipped. I looked up at the sky and the new day's sun nourished me. I closed my eyes. I listened to all the humans and their varying energies move and speak and be around me.

With a half-eaten doughnut in hand, I pressed my body against Chris and wobbled down the street toward our motel. It was barely noon. I had been awake for about thirty-three hours and my brain felt drunk. My eyesight streaked with light blues and pinks, creating my very own sunset filter on the late morning sky. I wanted more than anything to lay down, to stop the motion, and to sleep.

* * *

The next day I knew I had to move my body. After such an enormous effort, one of the last things you want to do is stay stationary. *"Motion is lotion,"* I heard the wisdom rumble in my ears. We walked a couple blocks to Coffee on the Hill, a local favorite in Leadville. Coffee and pastries in hand, we sat outside and watched the town come to life. Already the finish line was broken down, barely a remnant of yesterday's affair remaining.

My sister Sarah called just then. "Barbara! I signed up for my first trail half marathon!" She sang into the phone.

"Hell yeah," I cheered, "That's what's up!"

She had tracked me all day with her family, checking in on me from their cozy home in Cape Cod.

"It was wild," she told me, "We had a whole day of life and activities and then went to sleep and when we woke up – you were STILL running!"

A race like Leadville has a way of manipulating time, transporting runners to the past, projecting them into a desired future, and slowing them into the reality of the present. The finish line didn't just mark the end — it reflected back every version of me that showed up to run.

"It was wild," I coughed out a laugh. "I think I'm a different now."

40

I Know Who I am

It's no wonder
the thunder
rolls in me:
I am
a lightning streak
across a
mid–summer
night's sky.

41

Coming Home

Two days after Race Day

"I'm leaving tomorrow," I said into the phone. It was forty-eight hours after the race, and Chris was already back in Minnesota. I could feel him light up on the other end.

"You sure that'll be okay for you? You should rest," he said, half concern, half excitement behind his words. My lease wasn't technically up until September.

"I want to rest at home."

Home.

The word pressed its way into my mind, propping up its feet and getting comfortable. It stretched out its arms and took up space. I was ready for this word. I wanted this word. I was ready to go home—not just to Minnesota, but back to my whole self.

I packed my things, my car a game of Tetris. Sliding open the door to the back deck, I stepped onto the wood paneling. Pressing my hands onto the railing, I looked up one last time at the mountain shadowing the valley. A crow cawed. Chipmunks ran. And, out of the corner of my eye, I caught a lumbering beast slipping deeper into the trees.

A moose was leaving, too.

I took it as a sign.

Time to go.

I climbed into my car and puttered down the sloping dirt road toward home.

I had a feeling it would all work out. And somehow, it did. I had believed in myself. And I got to where I was going.

A belief is a thought we think over and over again, isn't it? A thought that becomes so very true to our being that life begins to shape itself around it.

Going into my big training runs, I was intentional about the thoughts I started with: *I am a mountain runner. I am an ultra runner. I am capable of big miles. This body is strong. I get stronger every mile.*

But during those runs—when things got hard—old beliefs had a way of sneaking in. As my body slowed on a steep stretch of trail, my first thought would be: *I'm weak.* The same belief that erupted at Twin Lakes, when I cried, "I'm not an athlete!" after climbing Hope Pass.

Sometimes we can shift those thoughts on our own.

Sometimes, we need someone to help us see what's actually true.

Often, in the middle of a memory, I'd catch another kind of thought—ones about my body, my worth, and who the world taught me I was allowed to be. Bit by bit, I reworked them. I reframed. I called in other voices when I needed them most. And in turn, I reshaped how I felt.

When I caught those doubts and chose beliefs that supported me instead of tore me down, I carried myself differently.

I am a runner.

I am an ultra runner.

I am a stronger, more confident woman.

I am still learning what my needs are.

I am an adventurer. I can figure things out as I go.

I am capable, and strong, and powerful.

And when I don't feel that way—I rest.

Like we all need to do.

Like we all get to do.

42

Re-framing

I used to be
afraid of bees
because a whole swarm
stung me
as a child.
But now
at thirty three,
I realize
that each bee
mistakes me
—simply—
for a flower.

43

Quiet Aftermath

Four days after Race Day

I have to water my plants was my first thought upon pulling up to my house.

After a two-day drive through Colorado and Nebraska, I was parked in front of my South Minneapolis home. Turning off the ignition, I sat in the humid car for just a second more.

In the 99-degree Midwest heat of late August, I collected my belongings and pulled them inside the house. No more mountains right outside the back patio. No more thin air or alpine bird songs or single-track trails alongside gushing waterfalls or encounters with through hikers with trail names like Chipper and Stump, Idaho and Limpy.

The next two months, I moved through the rhythms of work schedules and clear weekends. Of reading books and scrolling my phone and watching the world outside shift from summer breezes to copper-painted tree leaves. I attempted to write about what I just experienced and fought with the urge to let it all lay quiet, instead.

Chris and I slowly dated each other, holding hands as we strolled through the county fair, motorcycle rides where I gripped his waist and pressed my face into his back. We sat in the shade and sipped cold beers, just as we slowly drank each other in, too. We began to tend to our relationship in a deliberate way, like a couple of clock smiths peering into gears, tweezers in hand, delicate, with no intention of rushing, setting the project down when needed. We began to tick after some time, our hearts pumping blood back into the cracks we left there when I left earlier that spring.

I was different. And therefore, so were we.

Maybe you've heard about the Minnesota Goodbye: The "whelp" with a knee slap, the hugs, the walk to the door, the doorway chat, the 'We really should be going', the second round of hugs, the hand on the doorknob, the slow door open conversation that ends with "Get home safe!", and finally, the window wave. Over those two months, I gave my Colorado summer the Minnesota Goodbye. I'm certain Leadville told me to "get home safe" because that's how you say "I love you" in the Midwest: "Just be safe."

Safe.

Get home safe.

I swam in a kaleidoscope of big feelings post-race. I had days sunk into the couch, Netflix on but not really paying attention to the story line. I tried to run, even signing up for a fall marathon to "use my altitude lungs for," but my body sent me all the signals to slow down. Every time I tried to sit at my laptop to write stories, it was impossible to get my fingers moving along the black and white lettered keyboard. It felt like grief, the complicated and nuanced layers of letting something important go.

I once read that grief is "love needing a place to go." I loved every inch of living in the mountains. Of training for something mighty. Of connecting with like-minded people. Of completing a task that I set out to do. Of the spaciousness to heal something profound within myself. I've spoken with folks who have experienced something similar after weddings and giving birth, honeymoons and job promotions. There is a genuine let down after the festivities.

Yet, all endings bring forth new beginnings.

One cool Saturday morning, I pulled on my running shoes—not for a race, not for training. Just a jog. Just to feel the world move past me. I tied the laces, double-knotted, and stepped outside. A new me in an old place, yet everything was different. I started running, without a watch, without a goal to hit. I began again.

I like beginnings.

Always have.

44

Date Night

I like when we have big conversations
in small moments
the ones nestled between the roll of the die
as the trivial pursuit board laughs at
our not-so-youthful faces scrunched up
in competitive storytelling.
I like when beer slides past our tongues
and we loosen up enough
to bob our shoulders playfully to Prince.
I want to bump knees under the table
as the French fries drift past us
our nostrils flaring
like synchronized swimmers.
The waiter whose name
we can't seem to remember
never forgets a hello,
his smiley face tattoos
charming us every time.
I like trusting you with the car keys,

your night vision is better than mine,
and I get to keep my eyes on you
instead of the road.
If the night ends with me
in a thrown back belly laugh
and you leaning in to kiss me
then I know
we are doing
this right.

45

No Future Without Forgiveness

Five months after Race Day

I grazed my fingertips along the bookshelf in my office, looking for something to read. There, on the bottom shelf, was my copy of *No Future Without Forgiveness* by Desmond Tutu.

I had read it years ago. I remember how I shook with anger, teared up with sadness, and got a bellyache from the stories within those pages.

I flipped to the back of the book, and a pink highlighted line jumped out at me: "But what about forgiveness?" it asked. "It is perhaps the most difficult thing in the world – in almost every language the most difficult words are, 'I'm sorry.'"

A tear dropped onto the page. I turned to the next, and there it was again, staring at me like it knew something I didn't: "Reconciliation is liable to be a drawn-out process with ups and downs, not something accomplished overnight."

Just like training for a freaking ultra marathon, I thought.

Desmond Tutu partook in acts of forgiveness far mightier than the ones I was grappling with. A nation of war victims demands a reckoning far greater than one woman's healing journey. Still, his words met me right where I was. There was room for forgiveness. For the men I never consented to. For the failures of parenting. For the stories I believed about my own body. For myself.

I reached for a sticky note and pressed it inside the book. Drawing out a pen, I watched my hand write: "I love you. I'm sorry. I forgive you." I stared at the ink, the pen strokes smudging behind the tears welling in my eyes. I whispered the words aloud, trying them on like a new coat I wasn't sure fit yet.

"I love you, Barbara," I said, pressing my hand to my heart. "I'm sorry. I forgive you."

The hand was mine. But it belonged to all the versions of me—the little girl who got stung and spanked, the college student disoriented by shame, the young woman who kept going through every long run. The runner. The storyteller. The woman becoming whole.

Maybe we can't wait around for an ideal apology. Maybe, when the timing is right and the soul is ready, we exhale into forgiveness instead. We forgive people for acting from what they knew. We soften toward our past selves. We offer ourselves the radical act of mercy.

That hand on my chest was my own. The forgiveness I spoke was my own. And the future—well, it could begin with this: a sticky note, a breath, and a willingness to let go.

I looked around the room and marveled at the life I get to call mine. There I was, not dissociating or hovering above it all— but living it. Embodied.

I was a woman who let running carry her where she deserved to go. A woman who takes no shit because Leadville taught her not to. A woman who feels her body as a force of strength and purpose, not a thing to shrink or decorate.

Car keys in one hand, Chris's fingers in the other, I stepped out the front door into date night—to celebrate nothing more than the ordinary, beautiful act of loving and being loved well.

To my body: I love you. I'm sorry. Thank you for getting me through it all, again and again.

And thank you, Leadville. Because of you, I've found my way back home. To my body. To my self.

And that is everything.

46

I've Become a Person Who

I've become a person who
waves at rumbling trucks and cars
as I walk down a mud-dirt road;
drives in silence along winding
mountain passes and fir tree forests;
watches the sun play behind clouds
and dance back out to see me again;
goes to bed under a thick comforter
just to wake with the precious dawn;
takes up space sitting and standing
and roaming the local grocery store;
says "hello!" to birds
and "excuse me!" to groundhogs
and "good bye!" to each trekked trail;
laughs at the nature of dogs
marvels at the magnificence of moose;
savors easy mornings
is enraptured by starlit nights;
slides inky pen over paper each day

to make sense wondrous thoughts;
loses time in a book, legs resting
as a cat lays purring on me;
runs miles upon miles just to memorize
the holiness of earth's lush land;
listens for a moment at the rush
of thawed winter turned to stream;
forgets to look at her phone
and remembers to be here
really here
in this place;
I have become a person who
lives and breathes
as much as she is able.
I have become a person who
feels alive and well
and free.

47

Resources You Might Find Useful (I Did)

AllTrails App for trail mapping and discovery in Colorado

Insight Timer App for meditations and chill vibes

Zen Ren Healing Arts in Fairplay, CO for body work

America's Highest Gym in Alma, CO for strength workouts

At Your Pace Coaching with Greg Soutiea for running plans

Don Reichelt of Boundless Endurance for Leadville prep

Leadville Race Series for all race information

No Future Without Forgiveness by Desmond Tutu for a good read

Alma, CO for high altitude training and small town vibes

A blank notebook for creating your future

A willing mind for taking on new ways of being

A deep knowing within that the right people will arrive to support you

A growing relationship with your playful Inner Child

Relentless forward motion for a successful race day in the clouds

The decision to "talk back" to the negative voice inside you

Me. Reach out anytime. I am a resource for anyone endeavoring to run the Leadville 100 Trail Run for the first time. Or someone just trying to be a better human.

Epilogue

It's been two years since I've run the Leadville 100 and I am proud to report that I am going back to run it this year, 2025. I finished my final edits of my manuscript up at 9900 feet overlooking the town of Breckenridge as I acclimate once again to altitude. I'm remembering everything from that summer in a whirlwind whoosh.

A lot has changed since I first found Leadville (or rather, when Leadville found me). And so has so little. The summer of 2023 served not only as a training season for a lofty athletic goal, it also gave me room for important inner exploration. I especially reckoned with the relationship I had to my body, my mind, and how both religion and the way I was raised impacted those elements for me.

My parents had a hard time reading the first draft of this book, understandably. Here was one of their twelve children vocally denouncing the faith they raised her in, as well as being a little too real about what their parenting felt like at times to her little girl self. I am not here to tell their story, at least not right now. But, I am here to tell a part of mine and to tell it through the lens of both the child and the adult. I love my parents and I know they did the best they could with what they had.

I am a big believer in storytelling as a balm. It's a way to make good sense of the past and find a healing bridge forward. There is so much history, so many stories, and a wild amount of unknowns that will simply not be certain. We cannot know each other's full story. But, I had to write this book to make sense of my own story, as well as to protect and love the little girl and young woman I once was. I look forward to hearing more stories from my parents so that we can be better together on this tiny planet in a magnificent universe.

I'm learning more how everything is in motion and no singular event changes everything for the better. But rather, we can use each journey to learn more about ourselves and allow ourselves to be witnessed. I see this story of Leadville as a poetic case study on a small portion of my humanity. It's not the Gospel truth, nor is it pure poetry or hard science. It's just a slice of who one runner was on her way to and through a rugged one hundred mile course in Colorado in the summer of 2023. It's missing a lot, but it holds enough.

Running has a way of bringing me back into my body — I imagine many of my readers feel similarly. With every step of that two-mile-high summer, I began to understand what it meant to come back home to myself.

May we all have the courage to share the slices of ourselves. May we choose to bear witness to the vulnerable imperfections of ourselves and others. May we forgive ourselves, and our transgressors, so that life can sparkle and shine in the way that it's meant to.

Most importantly: May we turn our headlamps off and stare up at the "Scorpion Star Party" in awe, even as we struggle to breathe, even when everything hurts, even when we just want to crawl back into bed.

I'll see you on the trails during the next adventure.

Go be great.

About the Author

Barbara Powell, MA, NBC-HWC, is a holistic mindset coach and ultra runner. She is neither a mother or a nun, and that's okay. When not writing, reading, or running, Barbara's likely sipping coffee, playing BINGO, or enjoying a sauna. She lives in Minneapolis, MN with her partner Chris and their dog, Blue and cat, Benson. *Finding Leadville* is her first book.

You can connect with me on:

🌐 https://www.loveultrarunning.com
🔗 https://www.instagram.com/barbarapowellcoach